JACOB-ISRAEL

GOD'S MAN OF FAITH AND POWER

FRANCES SPILMAN

JACOB-ISRAEL
God's Man of Faith and Power
by Frances Spilman

Printed in the United States of America

ISBN 978-1-60266-093-9

www.xulonpress.com

"(ABRAHAM) was called the friend of God."
James 2:23

"DAVID, a man after mine own heart."
Acts 13:22

"JACOB have I loved."
Rom. 9:13

"DANIEL, a man greatly beloved."
Dan. 10:11

CONTENTS

Preface.. ix
Introduction.. xiii
Chapter 1   The Prophecy.............................19
Chapter 2   Reaching Out to Claim God's
                   Calling 23
Chapter 3   Meanings of Bible Names.........27
Chapter 4   Was Jacob a "Plain" Man? 35
Chapter 5   Esau Despises His Birthright......41
Chapter 6   Disqualified 51
Chapter 7   The Stolen Blessing?..................55
Chapter 8   Rebekah-A Remarkable
                   Woman.......................................69
Chapter 9   Encounter With God..................75
Chapter 10   Jacob and Laban 85
Chapter 11   Going Home to the Promised
                   Land...97
Chapter 12   A Humble Prayer for Help 107
Chapter 13   God Responds to Jacob's
                   Prayer 117

Chapter 14   When a Man's Ways Please the
              Lord 125
Chapter 15   Life in Canaan Begins..............131
Chapter 16   A Chosen Teenager...................139
Chapter 17   The Cost of Being Part of a Larger
              Plan..147
Chapter 18   Joseph Blooms Where He is
              Planted.......................................153
Chapter 19   Unexpected Change Challenges
              Faith...157
Chapter 20   Faith is Passed On 165

PREFACE

S ince my early Christian life I have admired the loveable and impetuous apostle, Peter. I am especially inspired by his faith and considerable courage when he stepped out of the safety of his ship, set his feet on the wind-tossed waves and started walking to Jesus. Matt. 14:29 says he walked on the water!

We are not told how far he walked, but it was far enough to be out of reach of the ship, and close enough to Jesus for the Lord to reach out His hand and catch him when his faith faltered and he began to sink. Jesus said, "You of little faith, why did you doubt?" I have never thought of these words as a stern, disapproving reproof for failure, but as a gentle, smiling word of encouragement: "You were doing so well! Why did you doubt? You could have done it!" I always thought Jesus was pleased that Peter had enough faith to try.

However, in my experience, Bible lessons usually refer to the failure ("he began to sink"), rather than the courageous attempt to exercise faith ("he walked on the water"). And the usual lesson is, "Don't take your eyes off Jesus to look at your circumstances." Good Lesson. But why are the positive aspects of Peter's action rarely if ever mentioned? He is an inspiring example to us to step out of the security of our safe and comfortable nests and attempt great things for the Lord. His success was temporary, his faith faltered, but at least he tried!

I began to notice that in most teaching about biblical characters the focus is usually on the negative more than the positive, on their failures rather than their faith. More is made of their negative qualities than of their important contribution to God's plan.

This is especially true about Jacob. I became intrigued with this fascinating man because in popular teaching he is presented almost always in a negative way, and his perceived faults multiplied and embellished. Rarely is his faith recognized, and very little is said about his central role in God's plan.

Was Jacob really as bad as they say he was?

We have fallen into the unfortunate habit of reading about biblical characters for the purpose of finding moral lessons from their sins, weaknesses, and mistakes. We make their sins more important than their faith. To read the Bible only to find moral lessons is to miss its larger message.

For some reason we humans find a strange satisfaction in dwelling on the sins of our spiritual forefathers. It is a modern day phenomenon that researchers and biographers have gone to great lengths to find all the "dirt" in the lives of our national heroes.

We have been well-informed about the fraudulent dealings, the sexual sins, the dishonest, self-serving actions of our great American forefathers. What a tragedy that the same thing has been done with our spiritual fathers in the Bible. The average believer is more familiar with David's adultery than with his greatness as Israel's king. And who has ever heard any good thing about Jacob's character or actions?

We need to think carefully about this question: Why would God choose him as the father of the people who brought to the world the knowledge of God? One popular Bible teacher wrote: "If we had been choosing a man to head a nation, I am sure we would not have chosen Jacob".[1] But God did choose him!

We need to read the story anew to observe God's relationship with him, and to discover why God's choice was a good one. There is instruction and inspiration here if we can remove our critical judges' robes and try to see the man as God saw him.

In order to understand the heart and spirit of Jacob, he must be placed in the context of the covenant which God made with his fathers and with him. God established His covenant with those who had faith to believe His promises: "Abraham believed the Lord, and he credited it to him as righteousness" (Gen. 15:6 NIV). This is the message in the stories of the patriarchs. They believed God's promises.

In this book I will attempt to present the positive side of Jacob's life in order to rectify some misunderstandings of his actions and to clear his name of unjust criticism. As we discover his real motives we will see a clearer view of his true character. An open-minded evaluation of Jacob reveals a man whose faith in God's promises, like Abraham, was the driving force of his life.

We need to take a fresh look at this man whom God loved, and with whom He identified Himself forever, as the God of Jacob.

I encourage the reader to read the Scripture given at the beginning of each chapter. Even if you feel you are familiar with the story, read that portion once more to better compare it with the discussion.

INTRODUCTION

A world-shaking event of eternal significance took place very quietly in the city of Ur, on the banks of the Euphrates River, when God called Abraham to leave his home and go to a place He would show him. In blind faith, Abraham obeyed, and "Operation Redemption" began. Out of Abraham the Lord purposed to make a people for His glory and as a channel of salvation to a fallen world.

> "By faith Abraham, when called to go to a place he would later receive as his inheritance, obeyed and went, even though he did not know where he was going"
>
> (Heb. 11:8 NIV).

In the land of Canaan many great and precious promises were given to this man of faith. Here is a review:

Gen. 12:2,3 (NIV)   I will make you into a great nation.
I will bless you.
I will make your name great.
You will be a blessing.
I will bless those who bless you and whoever curses you I will curse.
All peoples on earth will be blessed through you.

12:7 (NIV)   To your offspring I will give this land.

15:6 (NIV)   Your offspring shall be as countless as the stars.

17:4, 7 (NIV)   You will be the father of many nations.
I will establish my covenant as an everlasting covenant between me and you and your descendants after you for the generations to come, to be your God and the God of your descendants after you.

22:18 (NIV)   ***Through your offspring all nations on earth will be blessed.***

When as yet Abraham had no child and his wife Sarah was barren, and the promises seemed impossible, Abraham believed God and it was counted to him as righteousness (Gen.15:6). This revealed the principle by which man could be brought into right relationship with God. Here is the key truth, the central theme, in the stories of the patriarchs. The New Testament calls it justification by faith. It was revealed early in the Plan of redemption that God deals with us on the basis of faith. The promises began gradually with one son, Isaac, to whom the promises were passed on. To Isaac were given Esau and Jacob. Esau was rejected and Jacob was chosen as the seed through whom the promises would come to pass.

These covenant men of faith did not live to see the completion of the Plan of which they were a part, but the Plan continued just the same. Jacob, chosen before birth, to play an important role in God's eternal Plan, fathered the twelve tribes of Israel through whom God planned to speak to the world. Israel became the repository of the knowledge of God through centuries of time when the rest of mankind were lost in the darkness of idolatry. The history of God's work on behalf of His fallen creation was kept alive through this chosen people. To them the Law of God was entrusted; in them the true worship of the one true God was established. In a world of heathen darkness, one people held forth the light, very imperfectly; nevertheless it was the only light on earth.

As believers today are saved not only to enjoy the benefits of salvation, but also to present the knowledge of God to His confused and lost creation, so the patriarchs were called to make known this God to the world. Though this was not stated so clearly to them, it was implied in the words: "in thy seed shall all the nations of the earth be blessed." The knowledge of God began to be spread as God worked through them.

Their primitive altars were the beginning of their witness to the world, as surely as churches today throughout the world continue the witness they began. The great commission to take the gospel to all the world is not new. It began 3000 years ago when a few men, Abraham, Isaac, and Jacob set up their altars in the midst of heathen Canaan and worshipped God Almighty. They were the beginning of the vast movement of which we are a part. We need to see this larger picture and honor them as pioneers of the faith.

Eventually the Saviour was born of this special people, and then in a greater way all nations of the earth began to be blessed through Abraham's seed, Jesus Christ.

It was from the descendents of Abraham, Isaac and Jacob that we received the Scriptures and the knowledge of God. It is from Abraham's seed, Christ, that we receive eternal life. Every believer, every faithful church, every Christian organization and ministry, is a fulfillment of the promise to Abraham, Isaac and Jacob: "Through your offspring all nations on earth will be blessed."

These spiritual forefathers could not have foreseen all this, but they believed God in their time and were used by God to bring it about. Understanding themselves to be pilgrims and strangers on earth, they looked through a glass darkly to a better and heavenly country, and a city whose builder and maker is God.

The New Testament brings further understanding as to the meaning of the covenant promises made to the patriarchs. Ultimately they referred to Christ.

> "The promises were spoken to Abraham and to his seed. The scripture does not say 'and to seeds', many people, but 'and to your seed', meaning one person, who is Christ" (Gal. 3:16 NIV).

If we are Christ's, then we are also Abraham's children, and heirs of those promises (Gal. 3:29).

> "The Scripture foresaw that God would justify the Gentiles by faith, and announced the gospel in advance to Abraham: 'All nations will be blessed through you'. So those who have faith are blessed along with Abraham, the man of faith" (Gal .3:8, 9 NIV).

These are the birthright promises and blessings which Jacob believed and valued, and for which he struggled. They flowed through him and his descendants to us today.

CHAPTER ONE

THE PROPHECY
Gen. 25:20-23

The story of Jacob begins before he was born. After twenty years of marriage, Isaac and Rebekah remained childless. Concerned about the promise of descendents as numerous as the stars, Isaac went to the Lord in prayer about this distressing problem, and his prayer was answered. Rebekah conceived.

During her pregnancy Rebekah experienced unusual and troubling disturbance within her womb. In faith she sought the Lord to learn the meaning of these distressing symptoms. The Lord answered her prayer also, with an explanation which was a prophecy as well.

"Two nations are in thy womb, and two manner of people shall be separated from thy bowels; and the one people shall be stronger then the other people; and the elder shall serve the younger" (v.23).

Rebekah would have twin sons, each of whom would father a nation. The two peoples would be very different in character, and the one stronger than the other. This was fulfilled in the nations of Israel and Edom.

"The elder shall serve the younger."

Historically, the nation of Edom was subservient to the nation of Israel for a period of time. As it concerned Esau and Jacob personally, the New Testament informs us that this saying means that God chose Jacob over the elder Esau to inherit the covenant promises.

> "And not only this; but when Rebecca also had conceived by one, even our father Isaac; (for the children being not yet born, neither having done any good or evil, that the purpose of God according to election might stand, not of works, but of him that calleth;) It was said to her, The elder shall serve the younger. As it is written, Jacob have I loved, but Esau have I hated" (Rom. 9:10-13).

It is not within the scope of this book to deal with the subject of divine election; but in this passage, as it deals with our subject, Jacob's election refers primarily to his *role* in the purposes of God. In other words, he was chosen, not simply for his own benefit, but to be used by God for purposes beyond himself. What were those purposes?

In establishing His covenant with Jacob's grandfather, Abraham, God had promised to give him descendants as numerous as the stars in heaven and as the sand on the sea shore. Abraham was promised the land of Canaan as a possession, that he would be the father of many nations, and that through him all the families of the earth would be blessed. These promises were repeated to Isaac and Jacob. The New Testament in Gal. 3:8 explains that this promise refers ultimately to the Gospel and to Christ.

> "And the scripture, foreseeing that God would justify the heathen through faith, preached before the gospel unto Abraham, saying, In thee shall all nations be blessed."

Through Abraham's seed, Jesus Christ, the blessings of salvation would go out to all the world. Jacob was chosen before birth to be a link in this chain of blessing.

By human custom, the birthright was Esau's as firstborn, but the prophecy revealed that it was to be Jacob's by divine decree. God's word to Rebekah was a prediction regarding her twin boys and a revelation of God's Plan and intention.

The replacement of the elder by the younger according to God's deliberate choice is a common circumstance in the history of the chosen people. Abraham had pleaded with God to choose Ishmael, his firstborn (Gen. 17:18), but God overruled saying, "My covenant will I establish with Isaac" (17:21). Jacob's firstborn, Reuben, forfeited his birthright position by sin, and the birthright was given to Joseph (I Chron. 5:1, 2). Of Joseph's sons, Ephraim was chosen over the elder Manasseh; and David was chosen to be king over his older brothers. Solomon was chosen by the Lord over David's older sons. So God sovereignly by-passes human custom as He wills, and chooses Jacob over Esau. This choice was made before the twins were born.

Rebekah could not have understood all the details of the revelation concerning her sons, but she did grasp the basic truth that Jacob was to be the one to inherit the covenant promises. The covenant line of promise made to Abraham was to be carried out through Jacob. This revelation to Rebekah of God's intention to use Jacob rather than Esau in His Plan, must be kept in mind throughout the story of Jacob.

The book of Genesis is not simply a miscellaneous collection of inspirational biographies. It is necessary to remember that this is Covenant history, Salvation history. The lives of the patriarchs had significance beyond their own personal relationship with God. Their lives were recorded, not to be oversimplified into modern moral lessons, but to show how they were chosen and used by God in His vast and eternal Plan, which they did not fully comprehend, nor did they live to see its consummation.

CHAPTER TWO

REACHING OUT TO CLAIM GOD'S CALLING
Gen. 25:24-28

A curious incident occurred at the birth of the twin brothers. Esau was born first, and because the baby was red, or ruddy, and covered with an unusual amount of hair, he was named Esau, which means "rough to the touch". The name by which he and his descendents came to be called was Edom, meaning "red".

Jacob was born next and was named for the fact that his baby hand grasped hold (as babies tend to do) of the nearest object, which happened to be baby Esau's heel; so he was named Jacob, meaning "heel catcher" or "supplanter". This name had nothing to do with his moral character as is usually assumed; just as Esau's name indicated nothing about his moral nature. Esau was named for his physical appearance; Jacob was named for the incident which happened at his birth. Names in the Bible often have more meaning than ours today, but very few indicated the character or nature of the person.

Bible names more often have to do with the circumstances associated with the conception or birth of the person; see, for example I Sam.4:21. When the angel named Abraham's son Isaac, which means "laughter", it was because his parents laughed at the thought of two aged people producing a child, not because Isaac was to have a cheerful or happy disposition. Sarah also laughed for joy at the birth of Isaac. The name had no reference to his nature.

More often a name has reference to the *role* that person is to play in the Plan of God. Shortly before he became the father of Isaac, Abram's name was changed to Abraham, "father of a multitude", pointing to his destiny and role as father of the chosen race, and ultimately of all faithful believers. Rom. 4:11 tells us that Abraham is the father of all who believe. His blood descendants and his spiritual children of faith are as the stars and sand for number. Through Abraham's seed, Christ, a multitude have become spiritual children of Abraham.

The incident of Jacob grasping Esau's heel, and the name "supplanter" also had prophetic implications, signifying the **role** Jacob would play in the Plan of God. In light of the earlier revelation to Rebekah, the name was in fact a prophesy. The name Jacob did not denote his character, but signified that he was chosen to displace Esau as heir of the covenant. God would disregard the normal custom of the preeminence of the firstborn and establish His covenant with Jacob, not Esau.

The name pointed to the **role** of Jacob in God's purposes and foreshadowed the history of the nation which descended from him. The children of Israel would displace others as part of the plan of God; Israel would supplant the Canaanites, taking that land from its idolatrous inhabitants, and possessing it themselves.

Chosen for God's purposes while still in the womb, Jacob was born reaching out to claim that calling, responding to God, even as a new-born babe.

Mistakenly assuming that his name describes his moral character, our first impression of Jacob is negative, and sets the pattern of our thinking of him as a bad character. Thus all the other incidents in his life are interpreted in a negative light as well. His reputation and character have been colored at the start by the mistaken belief that a Bible name describes a person's nature.

Speaking of Abraham, Isaac and Jacob, Heb. 11:16 says, "God is not ashamed to be called their God". If Jacob means "supplanter" in a bad sense, why would God call Himself "the God of Jacob" throughout the Bible? Somehow we are seeing Jacob in a different way than God saw him.

Jacob-Israel, the man and the nation, have always been controversial. Is he a supplanter, or is he a "prince with God" who has striven with God and man and prevailed?

CHAPTER THREE

THE MEANING OF BIBLE NAMES

It is a common misconception that Bible names indicate the personality or character of the person, but this is rarely the case.

Most Bible names actually have to do with:
1) Circumstances surrounding the birth or the conception.
2) The role that person is to play in the history of God's Plan.

The twelve sons of Jacob illustrate this. (As taken from Gen. 29 & 30).

REUBEN
29:32

See, a son!
Leah felt that God had seen that her husband did not love her, and now she thought she would have his love.

SIMEON
29:33

God hears
Because God heard Leah was not loved and He therefore gave her this son. The name does not mean God hears Simeon, but God had heard *her* grief.

LEVI
29:34

Joined
Leah felt that now, having borne Jacob three sons, her husband would be joined to her.

JUDAH
29:35

Praise
This name does not indicate that Judah would be a praising man, but that his mother, Leah, praised God for this son.

DAN
30:6

Judged
The son of Rachel's maid, Bilhah. Rachel named this son because she felt God had judged in her favor by giving

her this child. This had nothing to do with Dan's character.

NAPHTALI
30:7, 8

Struggled

The son of Rachel's maid, Bilhah. Rachel had struggled, or competed, with her sister, and had at last had children, even though they were by her maid. Naphtali was not a struggler; Rachel was the one who had struggled.

GAD
30:10, 11

Fortune

This was Leah's child by her maid, Zilpah. Leah said, Good fortune has come to me.

ASHER
30:12, 13

Happy

This is also Zilpah's child. Leah named him this because she was happy to have so many children and that others would now called her blessed (happy). This does not indicate that Asher was of a happy disposition. It has to do with his mother's happy reaction to his birth.

ISSACHAR
30:18

Hired
Leah's son. She purchased her husband for that night from Rachel with the mandrakes one of her sons had found. That night she conceived Issachar. His name reflected the circumstances of his conception.

ZEBULON
30:19, 20

Dwelling
Leah hoped that now having born Jacob six sons, he would dwell with her instead of with Rachel.

JOSEPH
30:22-24

May he add
Rachel's firstborn. She prayed that God would add to her another son. The name had nothing to do with Joseph's character.

BENJAMIN
35:16-18

Son of the right hand
Rachel's second son, born later in Canaan, and named by Jacob. Rachel had named him BENONI, which means son of my sorrow, because she died giving birth. Jacob gave him a more positive name.

Not one of these names had anything to do with the nature or character of the person. Most of their names were memorials of the circumstances surrounding their conception or birth.

Here are some other familiar names and their meanings. None refer to the nature of the person.

MANASSEH Gen. 41:51	Forgetting Joseph's first son born in Egypt. He said God helped him forget his afflictions and his father's house, and to accept his place in Egypt as part of God's plan for his life. It does not imply that Manasseh was a forgetful person.
EPHRAIM Gen. 41:52	Fruitful Joseph's second son. God had caused Joseph to be fruitful in the land of his affliction. It does not mean that Ephraim's character was fruitful. Joseph was fruitful.
MOSES Ex. 2:10	Drawn out (of the water) Pharoah's daughter found him in the river and named him accordingly.

SAMUEL I Sam. 1:11	Heard of God His mother prayed for a child; God heard and answered.
SAUL	Asked Israel's first king. Probably his parents asked for a son, however, this name may have prophetic meaning also. Saul was the king Israel asked for and God gave. If so, it had to do with his role in Israel's history, not his nature.
ADAM	Man
EVE	Life giver It refers to her role in creation; she was the mother of all humankind.
ABRAM	High father This was his birth name.
ABRAHAM Gen. 17:5	Father of a multitude This name says nothing about his character. There is nothing in the scripture record to indicate any significant change in his character at that time. It refers to the role he would play in God's Plan. We are

told plainly why the new name was given: "A father of many nations have I made thee."

ISRAEL	Prince with God
Gen. 32:28	Because Jacob struggled with God and prevailed. His new name refers to his role in God's Plan of redemption: heir of the covenant and father of the chosen people.

JOSHUA

Jehovah is salvation
His role in God's plan was to "save" the children of Israel by leading them into the land of their inheritance.

JESUS

Jehovah is salvation
Jesus is another form of Joshua. It refers to His role as Saviour.

JUDAS (ISCARIOT)

Praise
Judas is a form of Judah, which means praise. Very interesting! Does his name describe his character?

JAMES   The New Testament apostle.
                   James is the Greek form of
                   Jacob! Does the name mean
                   James was a supplanter?

PAUL   Little
                   Little may have described his
                   physical size, but certainly not
                   his character or moral nature.
                   In this case, it also would
                   not describe the role of this
                   great apostle to the Gentiles,
                   which was of such immense
                   importance.

Anyone can learn about the significance of Bible
names by consulting marginal references in the Bible,
Bible footnotes, different translations, commentaries
or Bible Dictionaries. Rarely does a name describe
the character of the person; it more often signifies the
role of that person in God's plan.

CHAPTER FOUR

WAS JACOB A PLAIN MAN?

Gen. 25:27, 28

"And the boys grew; and Esau was a cunning hunter, a man of the field; and Jacob was a plain man, dwelling in tents."

There is more to this brief description than lies on the surface. This passage describes the kind of men the brothers became as they grew up. The prophecy had said they would be "two manner of people". Esau was like Ishmael, a restless roamer who loved the life of the wilderness, hunting with his bow. He was not the domestic type.

Jacob, on the other hand, was the responsible family man, who had no urge to roam, but stayed at home directing the family business of caring for the flocks and herds. While Esau enjoyed the wild, free life, Jacob was there, quiet, industrious, responsible. We will see how these traits are revealed throughout his life. Esau was the happy-go-lucky type, who could not care less about his birthright. Jacob was performing the duties of the firstborn long before he purchased the birthright. A birthright involves responsibilities as well as benefits.

"Jacob was a plain man."

It is surprising to learn that "plain", translated from the Hebrew word *"tam"*, has the meaning of "complete", "perfect" or "upright", according to Strong's Concordance.[2] "Tam" is the same word used to describe Job:

"That man was perfect (tam) and upright" (Job 1:1).
"Hast thou considered my servant Job, that there is none like him in the earth, a perfect (tam) and upright man?" (Job 1:8).

Of course, the term "perfect" when applied to people does not mean sinless perfection, for all men, including Job and Jacob, have a fallen human nature, but the use of the word "tam" clearly indicates a divine endorsement of both Job and Jacob as upright men.

Some Bibles note in the footnotes at Gen. 25:27 that "tam" means perfect. Commentaries also note this fact. If "All scripture is given by inspiration of

God" (II Tim. 3:16) then "Tam" is the word God chose to describe Jacob. This was His opinion of the man. This fact should be kept in mind when considering Jacob.

Gen. 25:27, speaking of Jacob, is the only place in the Bible where the Hebrew word "tam" is translated "plain". Evidently human bias has long influenced the translation of this word in Jacob's case. Perhaps the Lord knew the man better than the translators.

To illustrate the influence of human judgment, Adam Clarke, in his excellent commentary, acknowledges that the Hebrew word "tam", which the King James Version translates "plain", does indeed mean perfect or upright. However, substituting his own judgment for God's, he remarks: "In its moral meaning, it certainly could not be applied to Jacob til after his name was changed."[3] But, of course, scripture does apply it to Jacob long before his name was changed.

Some recent translations say Jacob was a "quiet" man. This can be an acceptable description of him, and fits his character as revealed in the story of his life. Some English definitions and synonyms of the word "quiet" are as follows:

Peaceable, restrained in speech or manner, gentle, mild, easy going, calm, reserved, steady, patient, even tempered

To describe Jacob as a "quiet" man is to say only good things about him. Whether "tam" is translated "perfect" or "quiet", Jacob appears to be more highly honored in God's viewpoint, than the traditional evaluation of him.

What is the significance of that bit of information that Jacob dwelt in tents? First, it can signify his quiet life as a homebody. That fact has sometimes been elaborated to indicate that Jacob was a "Mamma's boy". Looking at it from a different view, being a homebody could describe a domestic person, given to the responsibilities of home.

Dwelling in tents recalls what Heb. 11:9, 10 says of Jacob.

> "By faith he (Abraham) sojourned in the land of promise, as in a strange country, dwelling in tabernacles (tents) with Isaac and *Jacob*, heirs with him of the same promise. For he looked for a city which hath foundations, whose builder and maker is God."

> "These all died in faith, not having received the promises, but having seen them afar off, and were persuaded of them, and embraced them, and confessed that they were strangers and pilgrims on the earth" (Heb. 11:13).

Jacob, like Abraham and Isaac, had no permanent dwelling in Canaan, recognizing that Canaan was not the ultimate land of which God spoke to them. They thought of themselves as sojourners and foreigners on earth. They were looking for a heavenly country, a permanent home.

They saw through a glass darkly that the promises went beyond this transitory life. An old song expresses their attitude: "This world is not my home, I'm just a passin' through". The patriarchs were looking at things not seen, the eternal things. Dwelling in tents was symbolic of their faith in spiritual, eternal promises.

This is the clue to Jacob's character. He was a man deeply aware of the promises made to his family, and this was the motivating factor in his life. His whole life was lived in view of the covenant promises. Like Abraham and Isaac, he was a chosen vessel, appointed to play a preeminent role in God's plan of redemption.

"Isaac loved Esau because he did eat of his venison; but Rebekah loved Jacob."

Much teaching concentrates here on the evils of parental partiality. While this lesson has value, it has tended to divert attention from the major covenant truths which are the central message in this historical record. The dealing of God with the patriarchs was based on their faith in His promises; and this passage reveals Rebekah's faith.

Isaac's preference for Esau was based on a carnal reason; he liked the venison Esau brought home from hunting. Rebekah had deeper grounds for her love for Jacob. She remembered and believed the word of the Lord to her, which gave him precedence over Esau. She knew her younger son had a special destiny as God's chosen to carry on the covenant of Abraham.

She must have kept the oracle about her boys in her heart. Her preferential love for Jacob was not mere favoritism, a mistake made by some parents, but Rebekah had a word from God and she favored the one God favored. The basis of her love was spiritual, faith in God's revealed purposes.

In the stories of the patriarchs, many things are made clearer if we see their actions in the context of the covenant God was establishing with them.

This is not simply human history, but spiritual history, and the recognition of this covenant relationship helps us to see beyond a surface reading to a deeper understanding of their actions.

Chapter 5

Esau Despises His Birthright
Gen. 25:29-34

Did Jacob steal the birthright?
Did he cheat his brother out of it?
Did he take unfair advantage of Esau?

The answer to these questions is found in v34: "Thus Esau despised his birthright." This is the Divine evaluation of the bargain made that day. It is a statement of God's disapproval of Esau's action. Note that it does **not** say, "Thus Jacob cheated his brother out of his birthright."

The disapproval is placed upon Esau, but not upon Jacob. "Despise" means to look upon with contempt, to disdain. Esau regarded the birthright lightly, placing little value on it, and willingly traded it for a bowl of soup!

Since God censures Esau, not Jacob, we need to reconsider this incident with an open mind to learn why. Jacob was making pottage one day (a kind of soup or stew made with lentils), when Esau returned from hunting. Esau said, "Feed me I pray thee, with that same red pottage; for I am faint." To be faint does not mean dying. Its primary meaning is to be weary. Esau was tired and hungry, but he was not on the verge of collapse from hunger.

Jacob responded, "Sell me this day thy birthright." In answer to that proposition, Esau said, "I am at the point to die; and what profit shall this birthright do to me?" Clearly, this was an exaggeration. This kind of statement is called "hyperbole". It means an extravagant statement not intended to be understood literally. We use such speech today: "Let's go eat; I'm starving!"

Surely Jacob's pot of stew was not the only available food in Isaac's wealthy camp! The family encampment included many tents and many servants (26:14). Any of these could have supplied Esau's need. He could have obtained food from his mother, Rebekah. He could easily have satisfied his hunger without sacrificing his birthright. The Living Bible has caught the spirit of this exchange:

"Esau: Boy am I starved! Give me a bite of that red stuff there!

Jacob: Alright, trade me your birthright for it!

Esau: When a man is dying of starvation, what good is his birthright? (Gen. 25:30-32).

Expressed in modern vernacular, it is clear that Esau was not literally in danger of dying from hunger. So Jacob did not take advantage of his "perishing brother". We tend to give our sympathy to "poor Esau". He was cheated out of his birthright; Jacob craftily took advantage of his starving condition. The trouble with this analysis of the incident is that it is in direct contradiction of God's viewpoint of it. Can we afford to disagree with Him who knows the thoughts and intents of the heart? Not only does the Old Testament condemn Esau, but the New Testament describes him as having a profane attitude, which we should avoid. We ought to agree with God on this matter.

There is nothing to be found anywhere in scripture which condemns Jacob for buying the birthright, but Esau is condemned in both Old and New Testament for selling it. In God's eyes it was Esau, not Jacob, who was in the wrong.

"Lest there be any fornicator or *profane* person as Esau, who for one morsel of meat sold his birthright" (Heb. 12:16).

This passage calls Esau a "profane" person. We get our word, "profanity" from this word; however, the issue with Esau was not bad language. "Profane" is defined as irreverence, or contempt for God or sacred things. It means irreligious, unspiritual, secular, as contrasted with sacred. Esau was not of a spiritual nature. His interests were secular, the things of this world. He had no interest in spiritual matters.

"He was not profane because he sold his birthright; he sold his birthright because he was profane".[4]

I Cor. 2:14 explains the difference between such people as Jacob and Esau:

"But the natural man receiveth not the things of the Spirit of God: for they are foolishness unto him; neither can he know them, because they are spiritually discerned."

Esau was a natural man, an unspiritual man, who could not comprehend the things of God; they seemed of little importance to him. He regarded the birthright with its spiritual promises lightly, because he had no spiritual discernment.

Jacob, on the other hand, was a spiritual man, with a bent toward God, who grasped the deeper significance of the birthright promises which had been made to Abraham and his seed. His desire for the birthright was not based on material interests, as is wrongly assumed, but with a desire for the spiritual blessings in this family's heritage.

If we think only in terms of a material inheritance, we miss the point in the story. The inheritance of Abraham's family was about spiritual destiny. It is this spiritual heritage which is the issue here. Jacob was after that larger goal of God's plan and purpose, for which God had chosen him. Esau was not interested in God's plan; Jacob was.

One commentator has said: "Jacob's youth was one of untiring effort to secure for himself the birthright, which belonged to his twin brother, Esau."[5] This comment is typical of the unjustified and greatly exaggerated accusations made against this man of God. It goes far beyond scripturally revealed facts. Nothing in the divine record indicates that Jacob tried persistently to obtain the birthright. It is true that he desired it, for he was motivated by knowledge of, and belief in, God's word given to his mother before his birth. He also believed the promises made to Abraham and his seed.

We may safely assume that the whole family knew the story of God's dealing with Jacob's grandfather, Abraham. We may be certain that those promises had been carefully passed on to Isaac and his children. Abraham had been charged to instruct his children regarding the relationship of their family with the Lord.

> "For I know (Abraham), that he will command his household after him, and they shall keep the way of the Lord, to do justice and judgment; that the Lord may bring upon Abraham that which he hath spoken of him"
> (Gen. 18:19).

They had been told how Abraham had migrated to Canaan in obedience to God's call. They had heard of the promise of a son with whom God would continue His covenant. They surely knew the story of Isaac's miraculous birth to his aged parents. Isaac knew by his own experience how God had commanded his father to offer him as a burnt offering. Isaac had cooperated with that test of faith, and had been present when the angel stayed the hand of Abraham, sparing the boy's life, and renewing the promises to Abraham's seed. We can be sure these stories were familiar to Esau and Jacob, along with the covenant requirement of circumcision.

In Heb. 11:13 we are given a little insight into Abraham, Isaac and Jacob's comprehension of the promises:

> "These all died in faith, *not having received the promises,* but having seen them *afar off,* and were persuaded of them, and embraced them, and confessed that they were strangers and pilgrims on the earth."

These men were not looking for immediate earthly benefits. In spirit they saw promises of greater import than earthly Canaan and material possessions, this world, and this life. Jacob could certainly see that neither Isaac nor Abraham had actually gained possession of Canaan.

> "And (God) gave him (Abraham) none inheritance in it, no, not so much as to set his foot on; yet he promised that he would give it to him for a possession, and to his seed after him, when as yet he had no child" (Acts 7:5).

Think about it. Abraham, during his lifetime, received no inheritance in Canaan at all. He did not see the fulfillment of the promises, with the exception of his promised son, Isaac. The patriarchs were heirs of the promises, yet all they had in their lifetimes were promises. This is exactly why their faith was so noteworthy. They died not having received the promises, yet were steadfast in faith.

It is a common mistake to think of this birthright in terms of temporal, earthly benefits. It must be kept in mind that in this story much more is involved. All the world was to be blessed through these covenant heirs, the covenant which included carrying the Messianic line to Christ.

After all, Esau would not be condemned for despising a material inheritance. It was that special covenant relationship with God and its far reaching promises which he scorned. Recall once more the New Testament comments on this situation.

"When Rebekah also had conceived by one, even by our father, Isaac; for the children being not yet born, neither having done any good or evil, that the purpose of God according to election might stand, not of works, but of him that calleth; it was said to her, The elder shall serve the younger. As it is written, Jacob have I loved, but Esau have I hated" (Rom. 9:10-13).

Jacob's election was not simply for his own salvation, but for a special purpose, a specific role in

God's plan of redemption; just as David was a chosen instrument for his role in Israel's history, and Paul for his role as apostle to the Gentiles.

Did God's election of Jacob therefore mean that God arbitrarily deprived Esau of the birthright? Not at all. Esau was presented with a test. He was tested with a simple choice: his birthright or a hot meal, spiritual blessings (and responsibilities) or momentary satisfaction. The test revealed his profane and unspiritual nature. He was not the helpless victim of God's sovereign will that Jacob have the preeminence. He was given the opportunity to express his faith, to hold his birthright, and to claim the promises for himself.

Esau did not have to accept Jacob's proposition; he could have rejected Jacob's bargain. He could have said, "I would die of hunger before I would part with my birthright blessings!" Esau failed the test. Ironically, he fulfilled the prophecy himself by selling the birthright.

In this testing of Esau, we have an example of the perfect balance between God's sovereign predestination of events and man's free will and choice. The challenge has always been: "Choose you this day whom you will serve" (Josh. 24:15). We are creatures of free will. We have the privilege and necessity of choice. The pair in Eden had to choose. Moses chose between Egypt and God's calling. When Christ came, the people of Israel were faced with a choice. Both Judas and Peter chose. Some of these made the right choice and some chose to their loss.

All of us are similarly tested, and we are exhorted not to make the same mistake Esau made, and sell our inheritance in Christ for some moment of earthly satisfaction. Many of our choices are irreversible, as Esau's was. Later he tried to take back his choice and it was too late. Esau's supper that night was an expensive meal!

In view of all this, why do we take Esau's part as the poor victim whom Jacob "unscrupulously" swindled out of the birthright? Why do we stand up for the unbeliever and so harshly judge the man who believes God's promises? We should agree with God's viewpoint of these two men, and not justify the one whom God condemns, nor condemn the one whom God justifies.

Jacob is consistently accused of acting out of greed and materialism. Another writer describes him this way: "His focus was purely earthly — involving land, people, possessions, and power over others".[6]

However, the New Testament tells us something entirely different about Jacob's focus. Abraham, Isaac and Jacob were heirs of the same promises (Heb. 11:9). They all lived in tents, temporary dwellings, because they were looking for the city with foundations, whose builder and maker is God (Heb. 11:9, 10).

"All these people were still living by faith when they died. They did not receive the things promised; they only saw them and welcomed them from a distance" (Heb. 11:13 NIV). They thought of themselves as strangers and pilgrims on the earth. "Instead,

they were longing for a better country—a heavenly one" (v16 NIV).

This tribute to the faith of the patriarchs shows that Jacob, along with Abraham and Isaac, was looking for something beyond earthly land, possessions and power. They were all looking for a heavenly inheritance.

> "The whole emphasis in this great faith chapter in Hebrews is that the faith of the Old Testament worthies was not earthly, but heavenly."[7]

Not only this, but Jesus confirmed that they saw more than temporal benefits in the promises. "Your father Abraham rejoiced to see my day, and he saw it, and was glad" (John 8:56). The patriarchs saw far into the future that a Messiah would some day be born from their descendants, and they rejoiced in the salvation to come. In spirit they saw the day of Christ and were glad.

It is evident from the testimony of these passages that Jacob's interests were far more spiritual than he has been given credit for. The New Testament helps us correctly understand the Old.

Before we judge Bible persons and their actions, we should be careful to look for God's stated evaluation of the situation. In the matter of the birthright, He clearly lays His disapproval on Esau and He pronounces no blame on Jacob. I suggest it was Esau who was the materialist.

CHAPTER SIX

Disqualified
Gen. 26:34, 35; 28:8, 9

Esau's lifestyle of roving the countryside evidently brought him into contact with the pagan people of the land, and he married two of these heathen women, which caused much grief of mind to Isaac and Rebekah.

Since the Canaanite people were under the judgment of God, and their country promised to the people of God in the future, these marriages disqualified Esau from the Abrahamic promises. His Canaanite children could not inherit the promised land. His pagan wives were also a danger to the spiritual life of the family. In fact, the descendants of Esau did become idolatrous.

Esau became the father of the Edomites, who were bitter enemies of Jacob's descendants, the Israelites, throughout the Old Testament. The book of Obadiah is a prophesy against Edom for some of the serious crimes they committed against Israel.

The four Herods of the New Testament were Edomites who ruled Judea for many years under favor with Rome. Herod the Great ordered the slaughter of the children of Bethlehem in an effort to destroy Jesus, the rightful King of Israel. Herod Antipas had John the Baptist beheaded. Later Herod Agrippa killed James the Apostle. Finally, Paul gave his witness to yet another Herod, who was almost persuaded to be a Christian. The Herods were all of Edomite heritage, and all were enemies of the Plan of God.

It seems strange that Isaac had done nothing to secure proper wives for his sons. His own father, Abraham, had been deeply concerned that Isaac not marry among the Canaanites. A servant was sent to Haran to his relatives, to obtain a wife for Isaac. Rebekah herself was that wife. For some reason not explained in the record, Isaac had not done the same for his sons. If Esau's pagan wives were such a source of concern to his parents, we might wonder why Isaac, whose responsibility it was, had not taken action to see that Jacob had an acceptable wife. We are not given the answer to this question.

Later, when Esau realized that Jacob had been charged not to marry a Canaanite, and that his own wives displeased his parents, he tried to make things better by taking yet another wife whom he thought would please them. Instead, he compounded the error by marrying a daughter of Ishmael, who though a son of Abraham, was outside the covenant relationship.

Esau, being the unspiritual man that he was, just didn't understand the implications of relationship with God or His covenant. He had forfeited his right to the inheritance even before Jacob obtained the birthright.

CHAPTER SEVEN

The Stolen Blessing?
Gen. 27

The birthright entitled Esau, as firstborn, to a double portion of the inheritance and leadership of the clan, but in this special family much more was involved. The birthright heritage included all the covenant promises and the Messianic line to Christ. Esau was legal heir with the right to the blessing. However when he sold his birthright, scripture shows that Esau was selling his right to the inheritance and the blessing.

> "See that no one is sexually immoral, or is godless like Esau, who for a single meal sold ***his inheritance rights*** as the oldest son. Afterward, as you know, when he wanted to inherit ***this blessing***, he was rejected. He

could bring about no change of mind, though he sought *the blessing* with tears"
(Heb. 12:16, 17 NIV).

When Jacob bought the birthright, he was buying the right to the inheritance and the blessing which bestowed it.

According to the custom of that time and culture, a birthright could be legally transferred by sale. It could also be changed by the father, as in the case of Reuben, Jacob's firstborn son, who forfeited his birthright because of adultery with Jacob's wife, Bilhah. Therefore Jacob gave the birthright to Joseph (Gen. 35:22; 49:3, 4; I Chron. 5:1, 2).

In this covenant family, the inheritance involved all the promises made to Abraham and passed down to Isaac, by passing the firstborn, Ishmael. Among other things, possession of Canaan was promised to Abraham's seed. However the most significant promise was that the entire world would be blessed through his seed, referring in the ultimate sense to Christ and the gospel, which would bring salvation to the world.

It is these spiritual covenant blessings which are the issue in this history. It was not the material inheritance which Esau despised; it was the spiritual patrimony which he disdained. And it was not the material inheritance which Jacob was interested in; he was reaching out to lay hold on that covenant relationship which he earnestly desired and for which he was chosen.

It has been called "the stolen blessing" but the blessing was not stolen, and there is no condemnation of Jacob. While Jacob's lies and deception of his father cannot be considered morally right, neither can it be said that he stole the blessing. If Jacob stole it, why does scripture condemn Esau?

Both spiritually and humanly speaking, the blessing was not Esau's. By God's decree it was Jacob's. Nevertheless, on the human level, Esau himself made God's decree come true by selling his inheritance rights, which included the blessing. Esau no longer had a right to the blessing; he had willingly chosen to sell it. Jacob didn't steal it, he had purchased it, and now it belonged to him.

When Isaac summoned his elder son to make plans to give him the blessing, Esau, if he had been honest, would have acknowledged that he no longer had the right to it. Instead, he saw an opportunity to take advantage of his father's favoritism, and he set about to deliberately acquire the inheritance blessing, knowing full well he had sold it to Jacob. Moreover, he had morally and legally sealed the bargain with an oath (25:33). Now he was planning to break his oath. It would seem that it was Esau who was intending to steal the blessing from Jacob!

Isaac's part in this is more difficult to understand. It seems possible that he had no knowledge of the exchange of the birthright between the sons. If so, Esau also deceived his father by withholding that fact. But it is almost certain that Isaac did know the word of God regarding his sons before they were born, giving Jacob preeminence over Esau.

Had he forgotten this? Why was he acting against the revealed will of God? Why was he going to give the covenant promises to Esau whose children were Canaanites and could never inherit the land? Why was he allowing his natural affection to override the will of God?

Isaac's disregarding of the oracle of God, and of the fact that Esau had disqualified himself from claiming the inheritance by his ungodly marriages, started the unhappy chain of events in chapter 27.

> "The basic word of guidance that the family possessed as to the relation of the brothers in the days to come is found in 25:23, 'The elder shall serve the younger'. There is every good reason to believe that Isaac knew the word, and good ground for holding that the sons were not ignorant of it.
>
> Now Isaac, in preparing to bless Esau, is openly taking a step to annul this word. He and Esau are working in defiance of it. Though Rebekah and Jacob are using deception, it can at least be claimed that they were doing it in the interest of bringing the promise of God to pass."[8]

Isaac and Esau were moving to counter the stated will of God, while Rebekah and Jacob were working to uphold it.

Jacob is consistently characterized as a born cheat, with the nature of a conniving swindler, forever thinking in terms of grabbing for himself what belonged to others. However, an open minded consideration of chapter 27 shows that the idea of deceiving old Isaac did not originate with Jacob at all. The sacred writer has made it as plain as possible that Rebekah was the initiator of the plan. She was the one who happened to overhear the plan of Isaac and Esau, and came to Jacob with the counter strategy. It was her idea; Jacob did not think up the plan.

This is not to justify Jacob for actually carrying out the scheme, but simply to show that the deception was not a product of his mind. It is regrettable that Jacob has been characterized with such descriptions as a shrewd schemer with the nature of a liar, whose every thought was to defraud others. He is often described as crafty, materialistic, covetous and unscrupulous, with a mean grasping disposition. These accusations are extreme, untrue and unjust.

I suggest there is another way of understanding Jacob. Though his lying deception of his father shocks our moral sensitivities; and while he cannot be justified for that deception, a surface reading of the account has resulted in a misunderstanding of his character. A casual reading leads one to think Jacob was simply a greedy and unprincipled cheat.

It is prejudicial to assign the basest of motives to Jacob. Another way to interpret his actions in this situation originates in the inspired depiction of him at the beginning of the account as that of a "tam" man, not sinless, but upright. There must have been good reason for the inspired writer to describe Jacob this way, and it should not be dismissed. That divine evaluation of him should give us pause and cause us to think a little deeper before jumping to judgment.

Accepting God's description, Jacob was a man of "upright" character, believing the promises, desiring to inherit the covenant relationship as revealed to his mother, and attempting to follow the call of God on his life. Taken by surprise by Isaac's sudden and secretive plan to give the inheritance blessing to Esau, it seemed that the purpose of God was in danger of being thwarted, as indeed it was. Once given, the blessing was irrevocable, so the situation was critical, the crisis immediate. In this urgent moment of crisis, Jacob was persuaded by his mother, against his moral sense and better judgment, to take action to prevent the error Isaac was about to make. Though their method seems wrong, it should at least be considered that is was not a greedy, deceitful nature which prompted Jacob's actions, but concern for God's purposes. This should be given fair and serious consideration when judging his character.

Many a family has fought over an inheritance, but there is much more here than a temporal legacy. Through Abraham, Isaac and Jacob, God was to reveal Himself as the only true God. He planned to make them stewards of His Law and the Scriptures; and ultimately that the Saviour would be born through their line.

Believing in this covenant made with the family, and in the direct word of God regarding the two sons, Rebekah moved in faith to cooperate with the will of God. She and Jacob believed it, Isaac had forgotten or ignored it, Esau despised it, but Jacob wanted that relationship with God. Had Isaac been obedient to the word of the Lord concerning his two sons, there would have been no occasion for Rebekah and Jacob to intervene.

Although it is human to judge things on the surface, God looks at the thoughts and intents of the heart. No one believes it is right to lie or deceive, but I suggest that God was more interested in Jacob's faith in the promises and his desire for the purposes of God. The Lord forgives sin, but without faith it is impossible to please Him.

Disguised as Esau, Jacob took the prepared meal to his father. His three lies, together with the goat skins on his hands and the smell of Esau's garments persuaded Isaac that this was indeed his elder son. The blessing was given.

"Therefore God give thee of the dew of heaven, and the fatness of earth, and plenty of corn and wine: Let people serve thee, and nations bow down to thee: be lord over thy brethren, and let thy mother's sons bow down to thee; cursed be everyone that curseth thee, and blessed be he that blesseth thee"
(27:28, 29).

"The dew of heaven and fatness of earth, and plenty of corn and wine" speak of earthly plenty, That "people serve thee and nations bow down to thee" was not for Jacob personally, but reaches down the centuries to the Messiah who would descend from him, as in Num. 24:17, 19: "There shall come a star out of Jacob, and a scepter shall rise out of Israel....out of Jacob shall come he that shall have dominion."

The words "Be lord over thy brethren, and let thy mother's sons bow down to thee" likewise did not apply to Jacob and Esau personally, but to their descendents. The Israelites did have dominion over the Edomites for a period in history, but this particular statement also refers ultimately to Jacob's seed, Christ, who would be lord over his brethren, who would bow down to him.

"Cursed be everyone that curseth thee, and blessed be he that blesseth thee" (v29), recalls the original promise to Abraham, showing that Isaac is conferring the covenant promise of Abraham.

"Isaac had inherited the prophetic office that had been Abraham's (20:7). He would speak with extra ordinary prescience and authority. His words would not be mere good wishes, but effectual to bring about what they expressed."[9]

The blessing was a prophecy spoken in the Spirit, and imparted what it expressed. Although Isaac thought he was blessing Esau, his words were inspired. Unconsciously he was fulfilling the word and intention of God. No sooner had Jacob gone out from his father, than Esau appeared with his meal of savory venison, and the deception was revealed.

> "Isaac trembled violently and said, 'Who was it, then, that hunted game and brought it to me? I ate it just before you came and I blessed him——and indeed he shall be blessed!'"
>
> (Gen. 27:33 NIV).

Isaac realized what had happened. He had spiritual insight to perceive that the blessing was given with divine inspiration. He had intended it for Esau, and did not know he was blessing Jacob. However God knew, allowed it, inspired the words, and gave the blessing to Jacob in spite of his deception. His hand was upon the situation in every detail.

"Indeed he shall be blessed" was Isaac's recognition that the blessing upon Jacob was valid, inspired, and effective, and that he could not change it. He knew God had intervened. God allowed this little drama to proceed because He knew it would, in the end, result in His purpose being accomplished.

Isaac trembled with conviction that the Lord had overruled his mistaken determination to give the blessing and covenant position to Esau. Jacob's deception may have been wrong, but God used it to accomplish His will.

Although both Esau and Isaac often have been regarded as innocent victims of Rebekah and Jacob's plot, scripture places the blame squarely upon Esau for the loss of the inheritance. Neither was Isaac innocent. His intention to circumvent the will of God that Jacob inherit the covenant relationship was wrong also. The fact that Isaac did not thereafter reprove Jacob indicates that he recognized his error, that he was acting wrongly to Jacob to give what was rightfully his to Esau. Not only did he not censure Jacob, but shortly after, Isaac confirmed the blessing as he sent him to Padan-Aram to find a wife (28:3, 4). Isaac made his mistake right, yielding to the will of God.

Jacob had been concerned in 27:12, 13 that his deception might result in him receiving a curse and not a blessing. His mother was willing to bear any curse upon herself, so anxious was she to prevent the mistake about to be made. However, it is interesting to note that no curse was given. God did not rebuke her, and Isaac pronounced no curse on anyone.

Esau's reaction was to blame Jacob for taking away his birthright and his blessing. He cried with a great and bitter cry, but it was too late. His tears were not tears of repentance for regarding the covenant promises so lightly, but tears of regret, for as the Amplified Bible puts it: "There was no chance to recall the choice he had made" (Heb. 12:17b). Esau did not lose his blessing that day in Isaac's tent; he lost it on that fateful day in the past when he foolishly chose to sell his inheritance rights for a bowl of beans! We cannot blame others for the choices we make.

Those who now lightly regard the spiritual blessings in Christ, preferring the secular lifestyle or momentary satisfaction, will at some time, like Esau, bitterly regret their choice.

One writer comments on this touching situation:

"Who would not be moved by the anguished cries of a brother who has just lost his most treasured possession?"[10]

This commentator has disregarded the plain statements of scripture and interpreted this incident according to human sentimentality. The facts are in direct opposition to this author's comments. The birthright was not Esau's most treasured possession! Scripture says plainly that he despised his birthright.

Esau said, "Jacob took away my birthright and now he hath taken away my blessing." This was his opinion of the matter, but his view differed from God's judgment of the affair. It is significant that the sacred writer records no word of disapproval or reproof for Jacob.

There are several instances in the Bible when people of faith lied and yet were blessed by God. One of the most familiar examples is that of Rahab, the harlot (Josh. 2), who won a place in the list of the faithful in Heb. 11. When the Hebrew spies came to Jericho, she believed in their God and expressed her faith by hiding them and telling a false story to the King's men. James 2:25 also speaks of her, saying she was justified, not only by faith, but also by her works. Her works included her lies and deception which protected the Hebrew men and made possible their escape. She was spared during the destruction of Jericho, later married an Israelite and became an ancestress of Jesus (Matt. 1:5).

Another instance of lying which won God's blessing is found in Ex. 1:15-21, when the Hebrew midwives feared God and disobeyed the King's command to kill the boy babies they delivered. They lied, giving the excuse that the Hebrew mothers gave birth before the midwives could get there. God was pleased with the midwives and blessed them with families of their own. He saw their faith and willingness to protect God's people.

Corrie ten Boom hid Jews in her home and lied to the Nazis in order to protect them. Should she be condemned as a deceiver? Sometimes in a fallen world we are forced to choose between a greater and lesser evil.

It must be understood however, that these were unusual circumstances and do not constitute a license to lie. In each case they were protecting God's purposes.

I submit for serious consideration that while deception and lying for man's purposes are sinful and God does not approve of them, He saw Jacob's faith in the promises and his intent to protect God's covenant purposes. Abraham believed God's promises and for this was counted as righteous (Gen. 15:6). This basic gospel truth is introduced early in Genesis and is easily the most important truth in this history of the patriarchs. This faith is the heart of the Gospel and it explains God's relationship with Jacob.

God was pleased with Jacob's faith in reaching out and struggling to gain the inestimable blessing of the promises and the covenant relationship which Esau despised.

Does God approve of deception? Obviously not, however, since all people are sinful and fall short of

God's design, He looks for sinners who believe His promises. He accepts and uses us according to our faith, just as He did Jacob. It is not Jacob's sin which is the point in this account; it is his faith in God's covenant promises.

"It was by their faith that people of ancient times won God's approval"

(Heb. 11:2 GNT).

CHAPTER EIGHT

Rebekah-A Remarkable Woman

S ince the purpose of this book is to emphasize the
positive side of its Bible characters, rather than
dwelling on their faults, let us consider this remarkable woman. The portrayal of Rebekah is commonly
that of a mother guilty of leading her favorite son
to lie and deceive, and suffering the result of never
seeing him again.

Rebekah was not a wicked woman; she was a
woman of faith, a fact that often has been passed over.
She was specifically chosen by God to be the wife of
Isaac, and to bear the chosen seed of that generation.
Hers is a beautiful and significant story found in Gen.
24. Abraham sent his servant to Mesopotamia to find
a suitable wife for his son, since he was not to marry
a Canaanite. The godly servant's prayer for guidance
in this mission was answered in detail, convincing all
that it was God's will for Rebekah to be Isaac's wife.

She recognized the leading of the Lord in the situation and did not hesitate to go with the servant. It was a step of faith for her to leave home and family, never to see them again, casting her lot with the God of Abraham and Isaac.

Her faith continued to be manifested as some nineteen childless years passed, but she did not follow the example of Sarah and suggest a substitute mother to bear a child for Isaac. After Isaac sought the Lord in prayer for a child, Rebekah knew she had conceived in answer to that prayer. When she experienced alarming commotion within her womb, she too, went to God in prayer. He answered her petition also, revealing His will and purpose for the twins. She believed His word to her about her two sons, that the younger was chosen as heir of the covenant.

Her faith in that word accounts for her special love for Jacob. She loved both sons, but she gave her "Amen" to God's choice. All these indications of her character and faith, and of God's hand on her life, were the basis for her actions regarding Esau and Jacob.

We need not approve of what she did, but we should give her credit for her sincere effort to cooperate with God's purposes. It is well to note that neither Isaac nor God censured her for her part in securing the blessing for Jacob.

Evidently Rebekah died before Jacob returned home more than twenty years later. It is only presumption to interpret this as the penalty for her actions. She was a spiritually minded woman who recognized that Jacob should not marry a Canaanite wife, so she awakened her husband to the need for Jacob to go to Haran to obtain a suitable wife. This needed to be done, and the scriptural principle is that "a man shall leave his father and his mother and shall cleave unto his wife" (Gen. 2:24).

Many a child has grown up, married and left home to establish their own life and family. It is certainly not unheard of that a parent dies while a son or daughter is away at war or the mission field, for instance. Such cases cannot be judged to be the consequences of sin.

On The Controversial Intervention of Rebekah and Jacob

The conventional view on this subject is that since it was God's will that Jacob be heir of the promises, if he and Rebekah had kept their hands off and not intervened, God would have worked things out in His own way, and Jacob would have had the promised inheritance without having to lie or deceive.

Of course, God is perfectly capable of accomplishing His will without our help. However, in most cases it is brought about through human actions. Moses was saved to deliver Israel from Egypt by the faith actions of his parents. Israel was not delivered from bondage by prayer and faith alone; it was accomplished by the deeds of Moses and Israel's cooperation with God's will.

It was not the will of God for the Philistines and Goliath to conquer God's people, but David did not simply pray and trust for their enemies to be defeated; he took his sling and accomplished God's will!

There are certainly times when we should simply wait on God in simple faith, but more often we are to put action with our faith and begin to cooperate with His promises and purposes.

> "I can tell you that the great men and women of God—those whom God has used the most—have been those who believed simultaneously in the absolute sovereignty of God on the one hand, and on the other, accepted their full responsibility as though it were utterly up to them."[11]

There is an often quoted saying, "Pray as though it all depends on God, work as if it all depends on you".

Queen Esther and Mordecai fasted and prayed when they learned of the plot to kill all the Jews, but they did more. They intervened in the critical situation with human strategy to prevent this tragedy. Mordecai suggested to Esther that she had been placed as Queen for just that time. The wicked Haman, the enemy of God's people, was defeated and the Jews were saved.

It was God's will that David's younger son, Solomon, succeed him as king. However, the aged King David, in failing health, had neglected to make it publicly known. Adonijah, the son who was actually in line for the throne, took advantage of the situation to have himself declared king.The prophet

Nathan and Solomon's mother, Bathsheba, working together, intervened, going to the ailing king to warn him of the crisis. David immediately ordered that Solomon be publicly anointed king over Israel. Thus the divinely appointed man came to the throne (I Kings 1). Since it was the preordained will of God that Solomon reign, should Nathan and Bathsheba have simply trusted God to work out His will in His own way? Rather, God used them to bring about His purpose.

God often uses human instrumentality. God has made His faithful ones co-workers with Him in His purposes. We are privileged to be laborers together with God.

Throughout history the evil one has tried in numerous ways to thwart God's plan. The pattern of his agenda is often not recognized in many such incidents in the Bible.

The situation confronting Rebekah and Jacob was far more than a family crisis; it was an emergency of vast significance. The very eternal plan of God was at stake. Much has been written today about spiritual warfare and the struggle between the evil one and the purposes of God. The battle has been ongoing since Eden, but is often overlooked in the lives of the patriarchs. Though the conflict may have intensified in these last days, it was apparent in the life of Jacob, who was the principle player in the drama of redemption at that time.

His life has been so reduced to personal morals that the larger picture has been missed. Intent on what Rebekah and Jacob did wrong, we miss the real significance of the situation. Francis Frangipane has pointed out that we do not always see what is going on in the invisible world of the spirit.12

Through the influence of the age-long adversary of God's redemptive purposes, a totally unspiritual man, who despised the spiritual inheritance of God's covenant, was about to inherit those sacred promises. Satan almost succeeded in derailing the plan of God before it could be developed.

The inheritance about to be bestowed was much more than silver, gold, flocks and herds. Isaac's blessing and legacy involved the covenant promises made to Abraham, and Isaac intended to give those promises to Esau! Why?

Isaac was a spiritual man, a man of faith; his action seems out of character. However, more than one true servant of God has been deceived by the great deceiver. This seems to be the only logical explanation for Isaac's strange determination to pass the covenant promises on to Esau. There is more going on here than personal and family matters.

We may disapprove of their actions, but Rebekah and Jacob successfully defeated the adversary's attempt to abort the plan of God.

CHAPTER NINE

Encounter with God
Gen. 27:41—28:22

Esau hated Jacob because of the blessing his father had given him, and planned to kill Jacob as soon as their father died. Unspiritual people often resent those who enjoy the favor of God. Remember Cain. Rebekah was told by someone (we are not told who), of Esau's plan, so she called Jacob and warned him, suggesting he go away to her family's home in Haran, to Laban, her brother, for a while until Esau's anger cooled. She said, "Why should I be deprived also of you both in one day?"

Her fear was that if Esau killed Jacob, the avenger of blood, usually a near kinsman, could avenge the murder by executing justice upon the killer. She may have favored Jacob, but she loved both sons and did not want to lose them both.

However, Rebekah was still thinking in terms of the covenant, and was concerned for the safety of the chosen heir. If Esau had succeeded in killing Jacob, the promises would have been thwarted. Throughout history, the chosen people have been in danger of annihilation as the adversary has tried in many ways to abort God's Plan and promises. Rebekah was being led by the Spirit to warn Jacob and send him away. It was no coincidence that she happened to hear of Esau's murderous intent. God intervened to protect the chosen seed from Satan's plan to eliminate the heir of the covenant.

It was upon covenant ground that she approached Isaac. Since Isaac had not fulfilled his responsibility to arrange a suitable marriage for Jacob, she took advantage of the crisis to suggest that Jacob go to Haran to find a proper wife.

Evidently the idea had not occurred to Isaac before, in spite of the fact that his own father, Abraham, had taken special care to obtain a suitable wife for him (Rebekah was herself that wife); and since Isaac also was grieved with Esau's Canaanite wives, he was agreeable that Jacob go to secure a wife among Rebekah's relatives. Thus this vital principle of the covenant would be met.

Now he charged Jacob, "Thou shalt not take a wife of the daughters of Canaan." At this point we might expect Isaac to sternly reprove Jacob for having deceived him regarding the blessing. No word of reproof comes from Isaac. Aware now of his mistake in attempting to give the blessing to Esau, and submitting his will to the obvious will of God, he blesses Jacob freely once more. He had blessed him unwittingly the previous time; now he confirms that blessing as being rightfully Jacob's.

"God Almighty bless thee, and make thee fruitful, and multiply thee, that thou mayest be a multitude of people; and *give thee the blessing of Abraham*, to thee and thy seed with thee; that thou mayest inherit the land wherein thou art a stranger, which God gave unto Abraham." (Gen 28:3,4)

"Give thee the blessing of Abraham" substantiates that it is the covenant promises of Abraham being conferred upon Jacob. According to Gal. 3:14 Christ redeemed us so that both Jew and Gentile might receive the blessing of Abraham through faith, including the promise of the Spirit. Because of Christ's redemptive work we can be justified by faith, even as Abraham, and enjoy forgiveness of sin, the indwelling Holy Spirit and eternal life. Such are the blessings which would flow out from Abraham, Isaac and Jacob through Christ to bless all nations of the earth.

Two other promises are recognized: the multitude of descendants promised to Abraham are to come through the loins of Jacob, and the land is promised to him, though he is about to leave it for a time and spend twenty years in another country.

With the blessing of his father, Jacob set out to go to Haran, a journey of several hundred miles. As he traveled, while still in Canaan, he stopped for the night in a certain wilderness place, and there dreamed a glorious dream which confirmed his faith and sealed his covenant relationship with the God of his fathers.

He saw a ladder, actually a stairway, set on the earth and the top reaching to heaven. Angels were ascending and descending upon it; and the Lord stood above it and spoke to Jacob:

"I am the Lord God of Abraham thy father, and the God of Isaac: the land whereon thou liest, to thee will I give it, and to thy seed:

And thy seed shall be as the dust of the earth, and thou shalt spread abroad to the west, and to the east, and to the north, and to the south: and in thee and *in thy seed shall all the families of the earth be blessed.*

And behold, I am with thee, and will keep thee in all places whither thou goest, and will bring thee again into this land; for I will not leave thee, until I have done that which I have spoken to thee of" (Gen. 28:13-15).

God confirms to him the very blessings which men have said he stole! Consider the implications of this first encounter between God and Jacob. He is fleeing his offended brother, having deceived his father in order to obtain the blessing, yet God meets him to confirm the blessing and to acknowledge him as heir of the covenant! Why does God immediately bless him with no hint of disapproval? This question deserves serious consideration. God must see Jacob as an upright man. This is a covenant vision, showing truths of the covenant of salvation which shall flow out from Jacob's seed..

Jesus spoke words reminiscent of Jacob's vision in John 1:51: "Hereafter ye shall see heaven open and the angels of God ascending and descending upon the son of man." He seems to indicate that he himself is the stairway between heaven and earth, the God-man mediator, by which the breach is spanned, reconciling God and man. God's grace in Christ is shown by the angels as "ministering spirits sent forth to minister to them that shall be heirs of salvation" (Heb. 1:14).

Jacob was an heir of salvation, enjoying the grace and providential care and love of God. Let us analyze what the Lord said to him on this occasion. First there are covenant promises, followed by personal assurances.

"I am the Lord, the God of Abraham thy father, and the God of Isaac."

From this time forward, God is pleased to call Himself the God of Abraham, Isaac and *Jacob*.

The covenant promises are now confirmed to Jacob, and the basic promise made to his fathers is included: "In thee and in thy seed shall all the families of the earth be blessed". The blessings of this promise have come to believers today because of Jacob's commitment to God's covenant.

The remaining promises are to Jacob personally. "I am with thee, and will keep thee in all places whither thou goest". He is not alone as he sets out into an unknown future. Where he is going is in the will of God and He will be with him. This is not the last time such assurances were given him. The faithful covenant keeping God unfailingly takes Jacob's part in every situation. Such is the blessedness of the man of faith whom God chooses and loves.

"I will bring thee again to this land". Though he has left family and home, with nothing but his walking staff to call his own (32:10), he is a spiritually rich man, for he has the presence of God and the sure promises of God. Though he is alone and an exile, he is assured that God will bring him back to the land of the promise.

When Jacob awoke from his dream, his reaction was fear. Finding fault, some have said, "Perfect love casts out fear. If he was in right relationship with God he would not have been afraid. He had a guilty conscience."

It should seem obvious that God does not make this kind of covenant with someone who is not in right relationship with Him. Even the most godly people in the Bible experienced fear (godly awe) when confronted with the supernatural presence of God. It is natural for mortal man to experience reverential fear and awe when God manifests Himself. In fact, we are told that "The fear of the Lord is the beginning of wisdom" (Prov. 9:10). Jacob was experiencing Ps. 34:7: "The angel of the Lord encampeth round about them that fear him."

He was astonished at the dream, thinking God was in that place, that it was the dwelling place of

God and the gateway to heaven. In reverence for this first unexpected meeting, he set up a stone for a memorial, and consecrated it with oil. And he vowed a vow:

> "If God will be with me, and will keep me in this way that I go, and will give me bread to eat and raiment to put on, so that I come again to my father's house in peace; then shall the Lord be my God; and this stone which I have set for a pillar, shall be God's house: and of all that thou shalt give me I will surely give the tenth unto thee" (v 20, 21).

Jacob has been unjustly accused of continuing his "characteristic shrewd bargaining", this time with God Himself! But there is no bargaining here, only grateful acknowledgement of God's gracious promises. Jacob did not say, "On condition that you do these things for me, I will accept you as my God". Some translators and commentators note that the word "if" can be translated "seeing" or "since", and understand Jacob's vow to say, "Seeing God will be with me" or "Since God will be with me".

Jacob is humbly receiving God's promises, in faith replying: "Seeing you are going to do all these things for me, I also promise certain things to you." This is an appropriate response to God's promises. Note that his response is based upon his believing acceptance of what is promised.

GOD	JACOB
Behold, I am with thee 28:15	Since God will be with me 28:20 (NIV footnote at vs 20, 21).
I will keep thee in all places whither thou goest 28:15	Seeing you will keep me in this way that I go, and will give me bread to eat and rainment to put on 28:20
I will bring thee again into this land 28:15	So that I come again to my father's house in peace 28:21
I am the God of thy fathers, Abraham and Isaac 28:13	Then shall the Lord be my God 28:21

Believing and receiving what God has pledged to him, he pledges himself in turn to God. His response to the promises is the same response of believers under the New Covenant: "We love him because he first loved us."

Then Jacob added something to his vow that God had not mentioned. God did not ask a tithe. This was Jacob's free will offering from his grateful heart. Did this voluntary vow to tithe come from a greedy, grasping nature? Notice too, that Jacob is content to receive simply food to eat and clothing to wear. Does all this fit with the character of Jacob as we have been accustomed to think of him?

Focusing on what God said to Jacob on this occasion, we may fail to notice what is missing in this exchange. God makes no mention of how Jacob obtained the blessing. We might expect Him to deal with Jacob about that matter, but there is no word of reproof or disapproval, only confirmation of Jacob as heir of the covenant and promises of blessing.

In many other instances of sin in the Bible, disapproval and reproof is stated clearly. The Lord expressed His displeasure with Saul and sent Samuel to rebuke him for disobedience (I Sam. 15): "Because thou hast rejected the word of the Lord, he hath rejected thee from being king". (v23).

Nathan the prophet was sent to rebuke David for his sin and to pronounce the penalty for that sin (II Sam. 12). God's displeasure with Moses for striking the rock was plainly recorded, along with the consequences of that failure (Num. 20:8-12).

Numbers 12 tells of the Lord's anger when Aaron and Miriam spoke against Moses. Miriam was stricken with leprosy. Peter was reproved by a gentle look from the Lord (Lu. 22:61). Divine disapproval is clearly stated about Solomon for being led by his pagan wives into idolatrous worship (I Kings 11:4).

In view of these and many other instances where God's displeasure is plainly expressed, we might wonder why no reproof is spoken to Jacob, only acceptance and blessing. There is food for serious thought here.

The Lord was personally establishing His covenant with Jacob, and Jacob responded in faith and
commitment. As Abraham believed God's promises
and was counted as righteous on the basis of his faith,
so Jacob was justified by his faith.

CHAPTER TEN

Jacob and Laban
Gen. 29-30

His faith strengthened by God's visitation, Jacob continued on his way to Haran, assured that he was indeed chosen heir of the covenant, and that the Lord was with him. Being guided by God, he came to the town of his mother's family, where he just "happened" to meet Rachel at the well where she came to water her father's flocks. He wept for joy at finding his relatives, and perhaps in gratitude for God's continued manifestation of favor. He is shown as a sensitive man, agreeing with the earlier description of him as a quiet and home loving man with strong family feelings. Destiny had made him a wanderer; one day he would even be required to travel to Egypt, but for now he had found family and a home in a strange land. And he found something else, for he apparently fell in love with Rachel almost from the first.

Jacob was joyfully received and worked with Laban for a month, at which point Laban offered to pay him for his labor. Jacob offered to work seven years for Rachel's hand in marriage. She was younger than her sister, Leah, and very beautiful. Because Jacob had nothing to offer as the usual dowry, he offered his labor as payment. So great was his love for Rachel that those seven years seemed but a short time; and it was real love, lasting a lifetime, for he was a man capable of abiding love and commitment. In fact, at the age of 147, when Rachel had been dead many years, he died with her name on his lips and love for her still in his heart. (48:7).

The wedding day arrived, the bride was veiled, and it was not until the next morning that Jacob discovered Laban's deception in substituting Leah for Rachel. Laban's sly explanation that it was not the custom of their country to give the younger in marriage before the older, did not mask his real motives to marry off both daughters and to obtain 14 years of free labor from Jacob. He had somehow failed to mention this custom before this!

The usual and only view of this incident is that Jacob was reaping what he had sown; that this was the consequence for deceiving his father. Too much has been made of this.

It seems to be human nature to attribute the misfortunes of others, and sometimes our own, as retribution for sin. Some people struggle with this mistaken idea: Did my child die because of some wrong that I did? Did Bob lose his job because of some character flaw that God was correcting? Did the neighbor's house burn down because of some moral failure in their lives? To see life's trials and afflictions as the result of personal sin, Jacob's or ours, is a mistaken view of life.

When Jesus and His disciples encountered the man blind from birth, (John 9), the disciples took it for granted that this affliction was the result of the man's sins or those of his parents. Jesus corrected their belief by explaining that this did not come upon him as the result of anyone's sin. There was a higher purpose, that the works of God should be manifested when the man was healed.

Some of us have the same complex Job's friends had when they falsely attributed his misfortunes to his sins. They said he was reaping what he had sown, which was not the case at all. This kind of judgmentalism is a sad human trait which has especially manifested itself in interpretations placed upon the misfortunes of Jacob.

Some even suggest that Paul suffered imprisonment because he had formerly had Christians put in prison; that he suffered stoning because he had participated in Stephen's stoning. This kind of thinking is not helpful to anyone. Paul was suffering for the kingdom, not as the harvest of his past life.

Doesn't the Bible say God chastens His children at times? Yes, but not all trials are chastening for sin. Sometimes troubles are to test our faith; will we hold fast our faith in the face of loss or injustice or suffering, when the world comes crashing down around us. Not all discipline is the consequence of sin.

> "My brethren, count it all joy when ye fall into divers temptations (trials); knowing this, that the trying of your faith worketh patience. But let patience have her perfect work, that ye may be perfect and entire, wanting nothing" (James 1:2-4).

> "We glory in tribulations also; knowing that tribulation worketh patience; and patience, experience; and experience, hope" (Rom. 5:3, 4).

As believers today we rarely see our trials as the harvest of our past sins. What if Jacob's trials were like our own, not the consequence of sin, but to develop faith and perseverance, wisdom and hope? When he was tricked into marriage with Leah, this can be seen in a positive light, as testing and refining of his faith, rather than the reaping of sin. Such expressions as "What goes around comes around" or "He got what he had coming", or "He had to learn his lesson" all carry a subtle tinge of vindictiveness.

When trials come to believers, comfort is found in Rom. 8:28: "And we know that all things work together for good to them that love God, to them who are called according to his purpose". Can this comfort not also be extended to Jacob in his troubles? Must he be reaping what he sowed?

Perhaps it would be more true to see his experience as all things working together for good, because he loved God and was called according to God's purpose of providing a channel through which would flow the blessing of salvation to a lost world.

Laban's cruel and selfish stratagem tested Jacob's faith. Was God really with him as promised? "Why would God allow this to happen to me?" (Haven't you been there?) The test no doubt provided opportunity for patience and forgiveness, as well as wisdom to develop.

It also revealed some positive aspects of his character. His reaction to the injustice was typical of the quiet man that he was. He was calm, and accepted the situation without anger, submitting quietly to another seven years of labor. He continued to serve Laban conscientiously, so that Laban grew wealthy as his livestock increased under Jacob's expert care. Laban even acknowledged later that the Lord had blessed him for Jacob's sake. Jacob brought blessing to Laban.

After fulfilling Leah's bridal week, Rachel also became his wife.

"And he went in also to Rachel, and he loved also Rachel more than Leah, and served with him yet seven other years. And when the Lord saw that Leah was hated, he opened her womb, but Rachel was barren" (29:30, 31).

Reading this passage carefully, it would seem that Jacob did not hate Leah, as the King James

Version says, but as in v30, "He loved Rachel more than Leah." The New International Version clarifies this in v31: "When the Lord saw that Leah was not loved..."

However, the passage indicates that the Lord was displeased with Jacob in this matter; and surprisingly, this is the only time in his life when divine disapproval is actually expressed.

We can sympathize with the man, he had not wanted Leah, nor did he want two wives. But God had a plan, and He sometimes works out His purposes in ways that are puzzling to our finite minds. It was time for the chosen seed to multiply according to the promise. Could it be that God's displeasure with Jacob's favoritism between his two wives was because he was not submitting to God's providential ordering of his life?

Was Jacob's unwanted marriage to Leah God's way of chastening him for his deception of his father? Or was there more to it than that? Considering the long range result of that union, it is difficult not to see it as an important part of God's plan.

We are told very little about Leah, and tend to give more thought to Rachel. We do know that Leah desperately sought her husband's love, even as she realized she would always have second place in his heart. She was thrust, possibly against her will, into the eternal purposes of God, when her father forced her marriage to Jacob. However, she became a major contributor to the plan of God through her sons, especially Levi and Judah. Some of the most significant people in the history of Israel were descendents of Leah.

Levi was Leah's third son, whose tribe became the priesthood of Israel. The most influential man in Israel's history, and perhaps the world, was Moses, a Levite, who wrote the first five books of the Bible. Through Moses we received the Ten Commandments and the whole Law of God. This descendant of Leah changed the world!

Jeremiah, Ezekiel and Ezra were priests of the tribe of Levi; and John the Baptist descended from Levi and Leah.

Judah, from whose name we get the name "Jew", was a son of Leah. Judah's tribe became the leaders in Israel, and produced David and Solomon. Both Mary and Joseph were descended from Leah through Judah, and Christ Himself, in His human ancestry, carried Leah's blood in His veins. The Lion of the Tribe of Judah was Leah's offspring.

Rachel's contribution to Israel's history is more modest. Of course, her first son, Joseph, was sent by the Lord to Egypt in order to provide a haven for the children of Israel during the famine, and was therefore a significant figure. Joshua, who became leader of Israel after Moses' death, and who led Israel to victory over Jericho and all of Canaan, was descended from Ephraim and Rachel.

But Rachel left a special legacy for us who are Gentiles. The apostle Paul was of the tribe of Benjamin, Rachel's son. Paul was called as apostle to the Gentiles, and laid the foundation of Christianity throughout the Gentile world. He was as significant to Christianity as Moses was to Judaism.

Though the world has been blessed by the offspring of both these wives of Jacob, it was from the line of Leah that the Saviour was born. Surely this unloved wife was placed in Jacob's life for more than discipline for his sin. Larger purposes were at work in the situation. God was forming a people who would change the world, and Leah was an important part of that plan. God had more in mind than chastening Jacob when he set this woman in his life. They were part of a larger picture.

Of course, it was Laban's selfish greed that placed not only Jacob, but his own two daughters in such an unhappy situation. Later, the Mosaic Law forbad marriage of two sisters to one man (Lev. 18:18). The reason given is that it produces rivalry, which is just what happened with Rachel and Leah. In their competition to produce children, each wife gave her handmaid to Jacob to bear more children. It was a distressing situation for all concerned, but in seven years, eleven sons and a daughter were born to the four women.

LEAH	Reuben	Issachar
	Simeon	Zebulun
	Levi	Dinah
	Judah	

ZILPAH	Gad
Leah's maid	Asher

BILHAH   Dan
Rachel's maid Naphtali

RACHEL   Joseph
               Benjamin (Born later in
               Canaan)

The birth of Joseph, Rachel's first child, coincided with the completion of the fourteen years of serving Laban. During these years, Jacob received no wages, save for his wives. He had nothing to call his own, and his heart turned toward his homeland.

His contract fulfilled, he asked for Laban's release so he could take his family and return to Canaan. As any responsible husband and father, he was concerned to provide for his large family. "Now when shall I provide for mine own house also?" (30:30).

Shrewd Laban was not ready to lose a good thing. He acknowledged that the Lord had blessed him because of Jacob. His flocks had increased and he had become well off because of Jacob's conscientious care of his livestock. He urged Jacob to stay and name his own wages.

The promise of God was that He would bring Jacob back again to Canaan; but in spite of his desire to return home, lacking a definite word from God that he should go at that time, Jacob accepted Laban's offer.

It is easy to overlook the fact that at no time did Jacob express resentment or bitterness over Laban's unfair treatment of him. However, knowing too well his father-in-law's craftiness, he carefully names the terms of their agreement. He will continue to tend Laban's flocks, and for his wages he asks only for the speckled, spotted or striped young which would be born. These odd colored animals would be fewer than the regular colored kids and lambs, which would be Laban's. In this way it would be simple to tell which animals were Jacob's and which Laban's. Jacob's venture was in pure faith, trusting in the providence of God to cause the odd colored offspring to be born, which would be his.

That very day Laban shrewdly removed from his flocks all the odd colored animals and put them in care of his sons to pasture some three days journey from Jacob, who would care for Laban's normal colored stock. These would be much less likely to produce the striped or spotted young. Thus Jacob started this venture with nothing of his own and with every disadvantage.

He then devised a method meant to cause the flocks to bear more spotted or striped offspring. Peeling some of the bark off of saplings, he set these white striped rods in the watering troughs where the flocks bred. This was to cause their young to be marked with stripes or spots.

Modern science tells us that this idea of prenatal influence is an old wives tale. Why, then, did it apparently work in Jacob's case? The answer is revealed as the story proceeds.

Jacob had spent his entire life in the livestock business, and being experienced in animal husbandry, he legitimately used selective breeding methods to produce odd colored sheep and goats. However, no matter how knowledgeable he was in his business, only a small percentage of the lambs and kids would be vari-colored. By the laws of nature, most would be of regular color and belong to Laban.

However, God was with Jacob as promised, and his share increased phenomenally. He did not cheat Laban, but he did use his knowledge of livestock breeding. Jacob learned later, and so does the reader, that his success was due to another reason.

CHAPTER ELEVEN

Going Home to the Promised Land
Gen. 31

At the end of this six year period, a family crisis arose. Laban's sons were unhappy to see things going so well for Jacob. "Jacob hath taken away all that was our father's" (v1). Before we join Laban and his sons in accusing Jacob of cheating them out of their livestock. let us read carefully to see if we can learn the truth of the matter.

At this time, the Lord spoke to Jacob once more. What did He say? Did He reprove His servant for cheating Laban? Did He censure him for dishonest dealing? What was God's view of the situation? No word of reproof is given for Jacob's management of Laban's flocks, but words of assurance that the time had come to return to Canaan as promised, and that God would be with him as He had been in the past.

"And the Lord said unto Jacob, Return unto the land of thy fathers, and to thy kindred; and I will be with thee" (31:3).

Jacob now had a definite command to return to Canaan; the promised time had arrived. His first step in obeying the divine directive was to call for his wives to secure their cooperation in this move. Rachel and Leah went out to the field where he was keeping the flocks.

His explanation to them tells us what really happened during those six years. Laban had changed their agreement "ten times". In today's language we would say "He changed my wages a dozen times", meaning numerous times or repeatedly. If the agreement was for Jacob to have the speckled, then the stock bore speckled young. Laban would then switch and say the striped would be Jacob's. Then the flocks would bear striped offspring and Laban would change the terms once more. With every change Laban insisted upon, it always turned to Jacob's advantage. (Gen. 31:6-9 NIV) Reading further we learn why.

Jacob related to Rachel and Leah a dream in which he saw that the rams which were mating with the flocks were striped, spotted and speckled. An angel spoke to him and interpreted the dream.

"Lift up now thine eyes and see, all the rams which leap upon the cattle are ringstraked, speckled, and grisled: *for I have seen all that Laban doeth unto thee*" (31:12).

It was not the peeled rods which caused the flocks to bear varicolored kids and lambs; it was the fact that *God* caused the flocks to bring forth the odd colored young. Why would God do this? Because in His viewpoint it was not Jacob who cheated Laban, but Laban who dealt wrongly with Jacob! The God who knows all hearts saw the situation as it really was, and has told us who was in the wrong.

If Jacob's management of Laban's flocks was dishonest and cheating, why did God bless it? He would not have helped Jacob cheat. It is Laban who bears the censure of God, while Jacob is justified and blessed with no hint of disapproval. The Lord actually helped Jacob so his stock would increase.

In reading scripture it is imperative that we not jump to judgment, but read the record carefully to determine *God's* evaluation of matters. Our minds have been conditioned to believe that Jacob was a crafty schemer by nature, and we tend to forget that it is Jacob who is the man of faith in this story! It is Jacob who believes God and is favored by God because of his faith. He had received the promise at Bethel:

"I am with thee and will keep thee in all places whither thou goest" (28:15).

God was faithful to His covenant man of faith. The Lord keeps faith with His children of faith. What beautiful assurance for us who believe today!

Rachel and Leah put aside their differences to agree completely with their husband to leave Haran and go to Canaan. They were aware of their father's character and his unfair treatment of Jacob. They too had been used by Laban for his own benefit. When we read the record of their marriage to Jacob, we have to wonder how they felt about those circumstances. Here we are given a clear look at their feelings about Laban's deceit. They felt they had actually been sold for their father's selfish ends. According to custom the bride would receive part of the bridal price, but the wealth that had accrued to Laban from Jacob's 14 years of service, had never been shared with them.

"Are we not counted of him strangers? For he hath sold us, and hath quite devoured also our money. For all the riches which God hath taken from our father, that is ours, and our children's: now then, whatsoever God hath said unto thee, do" (31:15, 16).

This was a stand of faith on their part, and obedience to Jacob's God. Ready to follow His leading, they accepted the word of command, and committed to follow His authority over their lives. They made the choice to follow the God of Abraham, Isaac and Jacob.

United in purpose, Jacob and his wives, with their children, servants, and all they possessed, took advantage of Laban's absence (he was away shearing his sheep at the time), to begin their journey to Canaan. It says they fled. At the same time we are told that, unknown to Jacob, Rachel stole her father's gods or images.

Jacob has so consistently been judged to be a dishonest cheat, that every action of his life has been viewed in a negative way. It is assumed that he fled in Laban's absence because of a guilty conscience for having cheated him out of his livestock. But it is made plain in the record that it was not by dishonest manipulation that he came to possess flocks and herds, but because seeing what Laban was doing to Jacob, the Lord intervened in Jacob's behalf to increase his flocks. He had nothing to feel guilty about. In God's view it was not Jacob who cheated Laban, but Laban who took advantage of, and treated Jacob unjustly at every turn.

Learning that Jacob had fled, Laban and his men pursued and overtook the travelers several days later. The night before their confrontation, God appeared to Laban in a dream, warning him not to threaten or harm Jacob in any way (31:24); and it had its influence on Laban's actions.

This situation illustrates God's intervention on behalf of His own, as recorded in Ps. 105:8-15:

> "He hath remembered his covenant forever, the word which he commanded to a thousand generations. Which covenant he made with Abraham and his oath unto Isaac: and confirmed the same unto Jacob for a law, and to Israel for an everlasting covenant: Saying, Unto thee will I give the land of Canaan, the lot of your inheritance: when they were but a few men in number; yea, very few, and strangers in it. *When they went from one*

nation to another, from one kingdom to another people; he suffered no man to do them wrong; yea, he reproved kings for their sakes; Saying, Touch not mine anointed, and do my prophets no harm."

God protects His faithful people. Recall the experiences of Abraham and Isaac, and now Jacob; they all experienced this covenant care.

Laban's intent was obviously not friendly. "It is in the power of my hand to do you hurt, but the God of your father spake unto me yesternight, saying, Take heed that thou speak not to Jacob either good or bad." He had to be careful how he handled the situation. He didn't threaten, but he rebuked Jacob for leaving secretly, accusing him of taking his daughters like captives. Of course, the reader knows this is not true. His self-justifying speech ends with the accusation that Jacob had stolen his gods (31:30).

Again, the reader knows that Jacob did not steal the gods. He first explains why he left secretly. He was afraid that Laban would not allow his daughters to leave. Everything about Laban's character indicates that he was a shrewd, hard and powerful man, and that Jacob's concern was justified. As for the gods, he indignantly gives Laban permission to search his camp for anything which does not rightfully belong to him.

Unknown to Jacob, Rachel manages to conceal the images from her father, and Jacob is justifiably indignant that Laban would accuse him of stealing anything that was not his.

"What is my trespass? What is my sin that thou hast so hotly pursued after me? Whereas thou hast searched all my stuff, what hast thou found of all thy household stuff? Set it here before my brethren and thy brethren that they may judge betwixt us both" (v 36,37).

In the presence of witnesses from both parties, Laban searches Jacob's camp and finds nothing that is not rightfully Jacob's.

Now the grievances patiently borne during 20 years of injustice pour out in Jacob's indignant response. He has served Laban faithfully for 20 years, during which time Laban's stock has flourished. Jacob's expert care had been such that there were no miscarriages among the flocks; he has not even taken the privilege of using an occasional animal for table meat; and contrary to custom, Laban required him to bear all the losses due to predators or theft. Day and night he shepherded the flocks in all extremes of the weather.

The time table of Jacob's sojourn with Laban is given in v41: fourteen years of service for his two wives and six years for the livestock, during which time Laban changed the terms of their agreement repeatedly for his own advantage. The truth of the matter is summed up in Jacob's final statement:

"Except the God of my father, the God of Abraham, and the fear of Isaac, had been with me, surely thou hadst sent me away empty. God hath seen mine affliction and the labour

of my hands, and rebuked thee yesternight"
(v42).

It is clear whose side God is on. With much
bluster, Laban backs off and proposes a covenant
between them. It was a face saving device for Laban,
who claimed that Jacob's wives, children and livestock were all his! But he would allow Jacob to leave
because of God's warning.

Laban's words, "The Lord watch between me
and thee when we are absent one from another," well
known as the Mizpah blessing, is not a blessing at
all. In fact it has the opposite significance. It was
an agreement that neither would pass that place to
harm the other. It was a covenant of distrust, not of
blessing. Laban, who has misused his daughters, now
wants Jacob to swear that he will not mistreat Leah
and Rachel! But at least the parting was peaceful,
thanks to God's intervention on Jacob's behalf.

Scripture has described Jacob as a quiet man
(25:27); he is a man of peace and avoids conflict if at
all possible. He had no intention of ever coming back
to attack Laban. Now by agreeing peaceably to this
covenant Laban wanted, he works out the situation in
peace. God is on his side, restraining Laban, so Jacob
cooperates with God.

It is made clear that Jacob knew nothing about
Rachel's theft of her father's images; it is not clear
why she did so. We need to give her the benefit of
the doubt that she did not take them for the purpose
of worship. Evidently there was some benefit to the

possession of the gods which is not fully understood today.

In some cases, the condemnation of Jacob has been carried to ridiculous extremes. Here is a quote from a present day preacher of the gospel, which I sadly heard with my own ears:

"Jacob was a rascal. He wasn't worth a dime! One day he decides he is going to run off with everything he can. He loads down the wagons and steals all that he can, and takes off from his uncle's house."

This is a shocking example of the incredible judgementalism against Jacob, which is so common among many who read the account ignoring the plain record or deliberately embellishing it. The totally false accusation above would more suitably come from the lips of "the accuser of the brethren" than from a Christian believer.

Gen. 31 states in the clearest language, so that there should be no mistake in the mind of the reader, that Jacob gave Laban permission to search his camp in the presence of witnesses from both parties, and Laban found nothing that did not rightfully belong to Jacob. There were no stolen items in Jacob's camp, except for the images which Rachel stole, and Jacob knew nothing about that.

Why defame the characters of God's chosen and our spiritual fathers? What purpose is seved by making Jacob appear as dishonorable as possible?

CHAPTER TWELVE

A Humble Prayer for Help
Gen. 32:1-33:16

"And Jacob went his way, and the angels of God met him."

Blessed with the visitation of angels when he had left Canaan, Jacob is now blessed with their reassuring presence as he is about to return. The promise on that occasion twenty years before is being kept: "And behold, *I am with thee*, and will keep thee in all places whither thou goest, and *will bring thee again into this land*; I will not leave thee until I have done that which I have spoken to thee of" (28:15).

We believe angels minister to us who are the heirs of salvation, but they are rarely seen. Jacob was privileged to see his guardian angels; and this was not only an encouragement to his faith, but to ours. Though we don't often see them, they are really there!

> "Are they not all ministering spirits, sent forth to minister for them who shall be heirs of salvation?"(Heb. 1:14).

> "The angel of the Lord encampeth round about them that fear him, and delivereth them" (Ps. 34:7).

Jacob said, "This is God's host" or God's camp, so he named the place Mahanaim, or two camps. His band was not alone! The believer today has the same promise: "I will never leave thee nor forsake thee" (Heb. 13:5). Wherever we go, He is there to keep, help, and deliver from dangers behind and ahead.

Behind Jacob is Laban, who would have hurt him if God had not forbidden it; ahead is confrontation with Esau. How would Esau react after twenty years? God has assured Jacob that he is heir of the covenant promises. Esau has vowed to kill him, with the accusation that Jacob stole it all. The question must be settled: who is the rightful heir of the covenant blessings? Will Esau claim the inheritance as his? Will he carry out his threat to kill his brother? Or will he accept the will of God that the inheritance belongs to Jacob?

It is crisis time! Jacob is returning in obedience to God's directive. The issue must be settled tomorrow! He sent messengers ahead to Esau in Seir,

the country of Edom, where Esau has already established himself, and which would soon become his
domain. Jacob openly announces his arrival, with a
brief explanation of his twenty years of absence. He
has been sojourning with Laban and now has family
and possessions. His message is one of courtesy and
respect: "My lord Esau…thy servant Jacob"; and
ends with a request for peace: "That I might find
grace in thy sight".

The messengers return with the alarming report
that Esau is on his way to meet them with 400 men!
Perhaps Esau thought Jacob was coming to contest
him for possession of the land. Remembering that
the prophesy had said: "The elder shall serve the
younger", Esau may have gathered his forces to
defend himself against the possibility of attack by
Jacob. Both brothers were apprehensive about the
intentions of the other.

Jacob tries to make it clear that he is not coming
back to take over the land or to rule over Esau. He
is coming in peace. He does not want to fight his
brother. He has neither the intention nor the forces
necessary to defend himself. He prepares for the
safety of his party by dividing all into two groups,
allowing the possibility for one group to escape if
Esau should attack. Then as any man of faith would
do, he prays. Here is one of the most beautiful prayers
in the Bible:

"O God of my father Abraham, and God of
my father Isaac" (32:9).

Since it is the covenant promises which are at issue in this meeting with Esau, and since it is the covenant which is the basis of his relationship with God, he addresses Him as the God of the covenant, confessing his faith in the special relationship he and his fathers have with the Lord. He believes God's word to Abraham and Isaac, and to him. He pleads the command and the promise:

"The Lord which saidst unto me, Return unto thy country, and to thy kindred, and I will deal well with thee" (v. 9).

It was not his own decision to leave Haran, but obedience to God's command and God's timing. His kindred includes not only his father Isaac, but his brother Esau as well. His obedience now places him and his family in danger...his kindred is coming to meet him...to kill them? His prayer is deeply humble:

"I am not worthy of the least of all thy mercies, and of all the truth which thou has shewed unto thy servant: for with my staff I passed over this Jordan, and now I am become two bands" (v. 10).

This is not a prayer of special sinfulness or specific repentance, but simply the prayer of a humble, thankful man mindful of the grace of God. The most righteous saint can make no higher claim than "I am not worthy of all thy mercies". This prayer expresses the attitude upon which all true faith is based. God's mercies and gifts are all by grace and undeserved.

The material blessings are thankfully acknowledged. When he left Canaan he had nothing to call his own but his walking staff; now with wives, children, servants, flocks and herds, he possesses two bands. It seems unlikely he would pour out such humble gratitude for his material blessings if he had gotten them dishonestly.

Now the desperate request:

"Deliver me, I pray thee, from the hand of my brother, from the hand of Esau; for I fear him, lest he will come and smite me, and the mother with the children" (v. 11).

It is not for himself alone that he fears. Now all the "holy seed" are in his care. He realized the significance of these children, not just his own personal love for them as a father; but these were the seed promised to Abraham and Isaac, the beginning of the multitude promised. These children were the building blocks of God's Plan of Salvation, through whom the world would be blessed. The light of the world rode on those camels. Through the children of Jacob would come to the world the knowledge of the one true God, the revealed word of God, and ultimately the Saviour. Jacob could not have known all the details as they are now revealed, but he understood that God's covenant plan was in danger; and his prayer was in concern, not simply for his family's personal safety, but for the whole purpose of God.

If Esau were to kill the heirs of the covenant, all the promises would fail. The adversary has attempted many times and in many ways throughout history to defeat God's plan. Jacob's faith in the promises was being tested. He fervently pleads the Lord's promises to him:

> "And thou saidst, I will surely do thee good, and make thy seed as the sand of the sea, which cannot be numbered for multitude" (v12).

We might think of it like this: "Believing your promises, I place myself and my children in your care, to protect their lives, so they may indeed become a multitude as you have promised." Resting his case in God, he made practical preparation for the meeting with Esau. He sent generous gifts of his only wealth, his livestock, some 580 animals. These gifts were not intended as bribes, but were conciliatory gestures of good will, expressing Jacob's overture of peace.

Some have interpreted these gifts as motivated by the guilty conscience of a crafty schemer trying to buy off Esau's anger with his carnal planning. This is but another instance where Jacob's character and motives are judged in the worst possible light. It is just as possible that the idea of sending gifts to Esau came to Jacob as guidance from God during his time of prayer.

We saw at the beginning that Jacob was a quiet man, gentle and reserved. Now approaching his brother, he does so in wisdom and peace. He sent out no armed men, no defensive show of force, no demands, no claims to the land, only gifts of peace. It would be difficult to imagine a wiser approach to the delicate situation.

Jacob's practical preparation for meeting Esau has often been labeled as lack of faith. It is said he should have relied on faith alone to work out the situation; that he was always contriving with human strategy, rather than trusting God to work things out in His way.

First, this is contrary to our own practice. We believe God will supply all our needs...but we also work at a job to obtain those needs. We trust in God to keep us safe in our homes from intruders who would harm us...but we also lock our doors. We do exactly what Jacob did; we trust in God and take practical steps to protect ourselves. Anyone who has insurance is not relying on faith alone!

This is biblical. Strategy and faith were used together in many instances in scripture. When Nehemiah was building the wall of Jerusalem under opposition from enemies, we read: "Nevertheless, we *made our prayer unto our God*, and *set a watch against them* day and night, because of them" (Neh. 4:9). They trusted God, but they also built the wall with one hand while the other held a weapon. Half of the people wrought in the work, while others stood guard with weapons ready (Neh. 4:16-18).

Why build a wall at all, if in faith, we are to refrain from all human means to protect ourselves? Nehemiah and the people prayed, believed, and took such practical action as humanly possible to protect themselves.

It was right and proper for Jacob to do everything possible to safe- guard his family. Any responsible man would do the same. At the same time, he knew this was not enough unless God intervened, so he prayed and put his trust in his God.

Now, Jacob is nearing the border of Canaan, and the question to be faced, which God alone could settle, was this: Is Jacob an illegal supplanter as his name indicates, or is he the rightful heir? Esau is coming with 400 men, apparently to contest the issue. The matter must be resolved. Facing this crisis, that night Jacob sent his wives, children, and all he had, across the ford of the brook Jabbok.

"And Jacob was left alone."

Jacob has sometimes been condemned for cowardice because he sent his family ahead and remained behind, placing them in the position of meeting Esau first. It is true that he was fearful of the coming encounter, but there is nothing about Jacob to make us think he was cowardly. In his recent prayer, his fear was mostly for his family, the covenant seed. It is unlikely he would send them into harm's way while he cowered behind.

The more likely reason he stayed alone was to continue seeking God. There is nothing wrong with being afraid, especially if it drives us to our knees in prayer. Later, the following morning, the record says Jacob passed over before them and went to meet Esau ahead of his family (33:1-3). When the time came, Jacob led the way. We need to take into account the whole incident before rushing to judgment. He was not a coward, but wanted more time alone to continue his prayer with God.

And God met him that night!

CHAPTER THIRTEEN

God Responds to Jacob's Prayer
Gen. 32:24-32

Alone in the night, a "man" wrestled with him until the breaking of day, but was not able to prevail against Jacob. So he resorted to his supernatural power and touched the hollow of Jacob's thigh, putting it out of joint.

Who was this mysterious "man"? Afterwards, in v 30, Jacob realizes, "I have seen God face to face and my life is preserved." Hos. 12:4 informs us that the man was an angel. Jacob had an encounter with a heavenly being, who is generally understood to have been the pre-existant Christ. This angel was unable to prevail over Jacob.

The angel finally said, "Let me go for the day breaketh"; but Jacob held on tenaciously, even with his crippled thigh, and insisted: "I will not let thee go except thou bless me."

Whatever the meaning of this incident, it seems obvious that it is in direct connection with Jacob's earlier prayer for help in meeting with Esau the next morning. It was in response to his prayer, and had to do with the immediate situation, not with Jacob' personal character. God heard his prayer and came physically to further deal with Jacob's request and situation.

The crisis he faced that night had to do with the matter of the covenant inheritance. As the two brothers are about to meet, the question must be settled, once and for all, without violence. Do the covenant blessings belong to Esau or to Jacob? Is Jacob a dishonest supplanter, as Esau claimed? This is not simply a personal dispute between two brothers over a material inheritance. This situation involved God's everlasting covenant, His plan and purposes for humanity's salvation.

This incident has been interpreted as nothing more than personal biography of Jacob. However, it is a mistake to see all his experiences in terms of his personal character. Neither Jacob, nor believers today, are saved for the one purpose of transforming our character; but also to be used as instruments to further God's purposes in the world. There is much more to this incident than Jacob's moral character.

What was the blessing Jacob so fervently wrestled for? He needed more than protection from Esau. He wanted vindication from his name, Jacob, supplanter.

Jacob's plea for the angel's blessing could be understood something like this: "Lord, you have told me I am your chosen heir of the promises made to my fathers. But Esau claims I am a supplanter, that I stole the birthright and its blessings; and he has threatened to kill me. If I am the rightful heir, protect me and validate me."

Jacpb stood ready to enter the land of promise as directed by the Lord, yet his name declared him a supplanter. So the angel got to the root of the matter, asking: "What is your name?" Jacob answered: "I have carried the name and reputation of 'supplanter'. If I am a supplanter, why have you told me the promises are mine? If the inheritance is mine, then vindicate me once and for all." He refused to let his divine visitor go until the matter was settled. And he got his answer!

"Thy name shall be called no more Jacob (supplanter), but Israel (prince with God): for as a prince hast thou **power** with God and with men, and *hast prevailed* (v 28 KJV).

"Your name will no longer be Jacob, but Israel, because you have struggled with God and with men and *have overcome*" (Gen. 32:28 NIV).

The traditional view is that Jacob repented and prevailed over his deceptive nature. But look at that verse again. What did God say he had prevailed over? "You have struggled with your deceptive nature and prevailed"? No. The angel said, "You have struggled with God and with men and have prevailed"!

Throughout the years Jacob's name has been freely enlarged upon, and described as "crafty swindler", "tricky schemer", "unscrupulous cheat", "conniving deceiver". It is presumed that when he acknowledged his name, he was confessing to all these sinful character flaws. And this has been his unjust reputation.

There is nothing in this account which says Jacob repented of any sin, or that he was transformed in character at this time. This is purely conjecture. The encounter was not about his moral character, but about his right to the inheritance.

He needed to be cleared from the false reputation implied by his name. He needed for Esau to recognize this, so there could be peace between them. The Knox Translation of the angel's words gives more light on the meaning of the name change:

> "Jacob is no name for thee, thou shalt be called Israel, one that prevails with God." (32:38).

Supplanter is no name for such a man as Jacob, so the angel relieved him of this misnomer, and gave him a new name of honor. This wrestling was physical, as the injured thigh shows; but it was also spiritual.

> "He took his brother by the heel in the womb, and by his strength he had **power** with God: Yea, he had **power** over the angel, and

prevailed: he wept, and made supplication unto him" (Hos. 12:3, 4).

It seems contradictory. He had power over the angel, yet humbly entreated him for his blessing. His tears and supplication won him the blessing: a new name and vindication. "The prayer of a righteous man is powerful and effective." (James 5:16 NIV). Fervent wrestling in prayer and supplication by a righteous man has power with God and gains powerful results.

Carefully notice once more these words: "You have struggled with God and men and have overcome" (Gen. 32:28 NIV). "He had power over the angel and prevailed" (Hos. 12:4). These plain statements are invariably reversed to mean that the angel prevailed over Jacob. Various expressions have been used to describe what happened here: this was the breaking of Jacob, he capitulated, in fighting with God Jacob failed, he was defeated, and he finally met someone who could overpower him.

What does the Scripture actually say? Did the angel overcome Jacob, or did Jacob prevail over the angel? Strange as it may seem, it says plainly that Jacob prevailed over the angel.

Why was he blessed with a new name? Was it because, at long last, he was ready to confess that he was a cheat and swindler? Human reasoning has read that into the account. The reason stated is quite the opposite: "You have struggled with God and with men and have overcome".

This is in no way a negative rebuke for Jacob's past life, it is a commendation! He is commended as one who prevails with God and men. The angel's words have been interpreted as future tense: "From now on you will have power with God and men and will prevail". However, the angel's words are in past tense. Jacob's new name will be Israel, not because from this time onward he will be a transformed man and will prevail, but because he *has* prevailed.

All his life he had sought the blessings of the covenant and to follow God's purpose for his life. He had persevered through injustice, misunderstanding, and opposition because he believed and pursued his calling. His father would have given the covenant promises to Esau; Esau accused him falsely and threatened to kill him; Laban deceived him and took advantage of him for twenty years; yet Jacob's faith remained undaunted. Through faith he had prevailed through every test.

"It was by their faith that people of ancient times won God's approval"
(Heb. 11:2 GNT).

Today, we have the promise: "He that overcometh shall inherit all things" (Rev. 21:7). By faith Jacob overcame and gained his inheritance and God's approval. And so shall we! Not only this, if we, as believers, prevail and overcome, we are promised: "To him that overcometh...I will give a white stone, and in the stone, a new name written" (Rev. 2:17). By prevailing faith we too can receive a new name!

This midnight encounter is such a strange and unique occurrence that its meaning is debatable. The focus has always been entirely on Jacob's personal morals, so that it has been difficult to imagine any other reason for his experience. A fresh approach is in order.

After twenty years of preparation, Jacob stood at the border of Canaan, ready to actually enter into his role as heir of the covenant and founder of the nation which God would create from his descendants. However, his name Jacob (supplanter), challenged his right to this privilege and honor. Acknowledging his name to the angel was not a guilty confession, but a cry to be cleared from the accusation of his name.

The new name, Israel, was God's declaration to all future history that Jacob was approved and honored of God for his faith and power: Prince of God, who prevailed in response to God's calling and pursuit of God's eternal purpose. The stigma of his man-given name was replaced with the name which declares him rightful and worthy heir of the covenant promises.

CHAPTER FOURTEEN

When a Man's Ways Please the Lord
Gen. 33

The Angel went his way and Jacob walked out into the morning validated as the rightful heir of the Abrahamic covenant, blessed with a proper name of honor, "prince with God", "One who has power with God and men, and has prevailed". Through faith and prevailing prayer, he carries his new name as he enters into his new role and destiny.

He arranges his family, with the concubines and their children first, next, Leah and her children, lastly Rachel and Joseph. He leads them out to meet Esau and his 400 men! His dependence is upon God alone, for he has no such formidable army to defend himself.

Jacob was a "quiet" man, a man of faith, courage and determination, but he was not the fighting type. His meeting with his brother illustrates this quality!

"And he passed over before them, and bowed himself to the ground seven times, until he came near to his brother" (v 3).

One Bible teacher interprets his action in this way:

"As indicating his want of faith in God, not withstanding Peniel, mark Jacob's timid and fawning approach to Esau."[13]

On casual (or critical) reading of this verse, it might be natural to interpret his bowing as a "fawning approach". But with even a slight knowledge of the customs and culture of that time, a very different understanding of Jacob's actions can be inferred.

In that time and culture, bowing was a gesture of respect, as it is in some countries today. When Sarah died, Abraham, owning no property in Canaan, went to the people of the land seeking to buy a piece of property in which to bury his wife. (Gen.23). In the course of the negotiations, we read that twice Abraham bowed himself down before the people of the land. This was not fearful timidity on his part, nor was it servile. It was a gesture of respect. He approached these pagan Canaanites with respect to arrange a purchase. Bowing showed him a gentleman, using the common courtesy of the day.

The customs of Bible times need to be taken into consideration and understood before critical interpretations are hastily put forth. Jacob was facing a sensitive situation. He did not go cowering in a fawning manner; he came respectfully seeking peace with an offended brother.

After the mounting suspense leading up to this meeting, it is with some surprise that we read that Esau ran to meet Jacob, embraced him, kissed him, and they both wept. How to account for the change in Esau's attitude between his bitter threat to kill Jacob in chap. 27, and this loving reunion? Why did Esau greet his brother so cordially? Scripture does not answer this question. Did God perhaps warn him in a dream while on his way, as He had done with Laban? Had twenty years mellowed him? Had he come to realize that in his youth he had willingly…and foolishly…sold his birthright? Did the gifts of livestock, coming at intervals, perhaps relieve Esau's apprehension of Jacob's intention in returning?

What we do know is that Jacob's prayer was answered. There was no violence, all were safe, and the brothers were reconciled. God was obviously at work in the situation to protect the chosen seed.

"When a man's ways please the Lord, he maketh even his enemies to be at peace with him" (Prov. 16:7).

This principle proved true for Jacob. Esau politely inquired about the women and children in the company, to which Jacob replied: "The children which God hath graciously given thy servant". Jacob witnessed of God's grace at every opportunity.

When Esau tried to decline the gifts of livestock, Jacob responded, again in typical character, "Take I pray thee, my blessing that is brought to thee; because God hath dealt graciously with me, and because I have enough." He humbly acknowledges that everything he has came from God's gracious hand in his life; he saw all that he had as God's undeserved blessings.

Notice that Jacob did not ask for forgiveness from his brother. To understand this, it must be remembered who bears the condemnation for the exchange of the inheritance rights. The divine opinion expressed is that Esau despised his birthright and later, when he wanted to inherit the blessing, he was rejected (Heb. 12:16, 17 NIV).

Unless we can align our opinion of that transaction with God's, we will miss the meaning of much of Jacob's life. We will not be able to understand his blessed relationship with the Lord or his true character.

Some interesting things become apparent in this account. Esau had become wealthy with livestock and didn't really need Jacob's gift: "I have enough brother, keep that thou hast unto thyself" (v9). He had become powerful enough to have 400 followers. The loss of the inheritance did not leave "poor Esau" a pauper to eke out a meager living because Jacob took it all.

Esau had already established himself in Seir (Edom), but he evidently lived also in Canaan where several of his sons were born (36:5). At some time after Jacob returned, Esau withdrew entirely from Canaan. Both brothers became so prosperous in livestock that the land could not support them both. The arrangement was peaceful and friendly (36:5-8). Read this chapter for an interesting history of Esau and his descendents. Jacob and Esau came together to bury their father when Isaac died (35:29).

Although God chose to give the land of Canaan to Jacob's descendants, He also gave the land of Edom to Esau. Several hundred years later, when the people of Israel were on their way from Egypt to Canaan, God warned them:

> "Ye are to pass through the coast of your brethren the children of Esau, which dwell in Seir; and they shall be afraid of you: take ye good heed unto yourselves therefore: meddle not with them; for I will not give you of their land, no, not so much as a foot breadth; because I have given mount Seir unto Esau for a possession" (Deut. 2:4, 5).

To Jacob went the land of the covenant promise; but Esau was given a land also for his descendants. God is merciful and just.

In his vow to God when he had left Canaan 20 years before (28:20, 21) Jacob had expressed his desire to come again to his father's house *in peace*. His request was granted in a most remarkable way with Esau's surprising change of heart.

CHAPTER FIFTEEN

Life in Canaan Begins
Gen. 33:18-20
Gen 34 & 35

G od had directed, "Return to the land of thy fathers and to thy kindred, and I will be with thee". Jacob has obeyed and God has kept His promise; Jacob's prayer for protection from Esau has been wonderfully answered. The brothers parted in peace and Esau returned to Seir, while Jacob continued toward Canaan. Chap. 33:18 marks his arrival in his homeland:

"After Jacob came from Padan-Aram, he arrived safely at the city of Shechem in Canaan, and camped within sight of the city" (NIV).

This was the first place Abraham had camped when he originally came to Canaan. It was there the Lord appeared to him for the first time in the land; and he had built an altar there to the Lord (12:6,7), so it was natural for Jacob to camp there.

Purchasing the land on which he camped, he also erected an altar to El-el-o-he-Israel, which means God, the God of Israel, using his new name. His last act before leaving Canaan 20 years before had been to anoint a memorial pillar to the God who met him at Bethel with the promise: "Behold, I am with thee, and will keep thee in all places whether thou goest, and will bring thee again unto this land." Now his first act upon returning was to build an altar to the God who had indeed been with him all those years of exile, and who had now brought him safely back as promised.

In light of the tragic violation of his daughter, Dinah, in Chap. 34, Jacob is usually condemned for camping near the city. It is interesting how we use a different standard in judging Jacob than we use in judging ourselves! Many moral lessons are drawn as to the evils of "camping near the city." With each such lesson we condemn ourselves! Do we not all live near or actually in the midst of an ungodly society?

The charge that he put his family in temptation's way begs the question: Do we live where our sons and daughters are exposed to physical danger and sinful influences?

Are believers to physically and geographically separate ourselves from unbelievers and have no dealings with them at all? Jesus prayed: "My prayer is not that you take them out of the world, but that you protect them from the evil one" (John 17:15 NIV). How can we be a light to the world if we don't live in the world? We are to be IN the world, but not OF the world.

Paul agrees when he writes to the Corinthians: "In the letter that I wrote you I told you not to associate with immoral people. Now I did not mean pagans who are immoral or greedy or are thieves, or who worship idols. To avoid them you would have to get out of the world completely" (I Cor. 5:9, 10 GNT).

There is no way for us to avoid unbelievers in this world. Jacob was in the same situation. We do have many Christians in our society and we have the fellowship of our churches. Jacob's family were the only believers, the only worshipers of the true God in the whole world. There was no place he could live and not be near ungodly people.

And Jacob did shine his light in that place; like Abraham he built an altar to the Almighty God and worshiped there, in witness to the idolaters in Shechem!

There is nothing in the record to indicate there was any socialization with the Shechemites, with the exception of Jacob's daughter, Dinah.

This naïve young girl...perhaps 14 or 15 at the time...made the very unwise mistake of going alone into the town "to see the daughters of the land." The young prince of the town was attracted to her and "defiled" her. There is some difference of opinion whether Dinah was seduced or raped, but young Shechem fell in love with her and "spoke tenderly to her." "He was delighted with Jacob's daughter" (34:19 NIV). He appealed to his father to get her for him in marriage.

Jacob heard what had happened to Dinah, but wisely held his peace; refraining from acting on the situation until his sons came in from the fields where they were herding their livestock. He was faced with a sensitive and volatile situation. A stranger in a strange land, he was in no position to arouse the hostility of his neighbors. Following the example of Abraham and Isaac, he tried to live in peace with the people of the land. He was not a man of impetuous action. The situation called for great wisdom.

The ten sons (Joseph was still a child and Benjamin not yet born), were justifiably angry that their sister had been violated. The father of the young prince appealed to them to allow the marriage and to live among the Shechemites, intermarrying and becoming one people, a temptation which exists among believers even today. Young Shechem offered any amount of dowry if he could marry Dinah. He was apparently sincere in his love for her.

The brothers answered them "deceitfully" (v13), pretending to go along with the proposal. They explained they could not allow their sister to marry anyone uncircumcised, but if all the males in the town would consent to circumcision, they would agree to intermarry and live among them.

All the men in the town were persuaded to be circumcised. However, on the third day when their pain was debilitating, Simeon and Levi, full brothers to Dinah, entered the city, massacred all the men and took Dinah home. The sons of Jacob then looted the town. It is unclear whether this was done by all the sons or only Simeon and Levi; but it was these two who were rebuked by Jacob.

In their anger, the two sons evidently overruled their father and took matters into their own hands behind his back. The record indicates he did not know of their plan until too late.

Jacob was very angry with his sons, and rebuking them, he said they had made him and his people to "stink" among the inhabitants of the land (v30). Their cruel and deceitful vengeance brought dishonor upon the people of God and upon their God. They had also used the sacred sign of the covenant in their deceitful action. They slew a whole town of innocent men for the guilt of one impetuous and lustful young man.

Jacob not only expressed his strong disapproval to Simeon and Levi, but their unconscionable act caused him to deprive them of their place in the line of inheritance. Years later, when giving his deathbed blessing to his sons, we learn how seriously he regarded their actions:

"Simeon and Levi are brothers...their swords are weapons of violence. Let me not enter into their council, let me not join their assembly, for they killed men in their anger and hamstrung oxen as they pleased. Cursed be their anger, so fierce, and their fury so cruel! I will scatter them in Jacob and disperse them in Israel" (49:5-7 NIV).

Jacob was disturbed with them for another reason also. It was likely that the surrounding towns would band together and take their own vengeance upon Jacob's people. He was very aware that being few in number, he could never withstand a united assault by the Canaanites. The chosen people were put in jeopardy by the treacherous cruelty of Simeon and Levi. The sin was grave and the consequences fearful.

Chapter 35 opens with the crisis brought on by the brothers' sinful actions. The chosen family was in peril; and in keeping with His faithfulness, the Lord once more spoke words of guidance, directing Jacob to leave the vicinity of Shechem and go to Bethel. There he was to build an altar to the God who had appeared to him in that place so long ago when he was fleeing from Esau.

In preparation for this move, Jacob ordered an outward and inward cleansing of his people. They were to surrender any strange gods or idolatrous objects they might have. He buried these things and left them behind. We may safely assume that Rachel relinquished her father's images at this time.

As they journeyed toward Bethel, God caused a great terror to fall upon all the cities around them, so they did not pursue after Jacob's company. Simeon and Levi's rash action had brought the plan of God into jeopardy, but God's supernatural protection saved them once again from almost certain annihilation. This was one more attempt by the adversary to destroy God's people and God's plan. It is another instance of God's faithfulness to His covenant people.

At Bethel the Lord again appeared to Jacob-Israel and blessed him, reiterating his new name, "Israel". The covenant promises are repeated that a nation and company of nations would come from Jacob's loins. Kings would come from his descendants, and the promise of the land confirmed once more.

In spite of these personal and inspiring encounters with the Lord, Jacob's life was a series of crises and afflictions which tried his faith and brought sorrow into his life. As he made his way toward Hebron where his father lived, Rachel went into hard labor and died giving birth to Benjamin. She named him Benoni, son of my sorrow, but Jacob changed that to Benjamin, son of the right hand.

Two unwarranted views have been offered regarding Rachel's untimely death. Earlier when she had grieved because she bore no children, she had said to Jacob, "Give me children or else I die." Some have surmised that because of these words and attitude, she did indeed die giving birth to her second son. Others theorize that she died because she stole her father's images. Neither opinion is justified. Scripture gives no hint that her death was the consequence of anything in her past. Why does human nature take satisfaction in thinking that Bible people suffered such penalties for past misdeeds? Do we judge our own misfortunes in this way? Her death was tragic, but not judicial.

Not long after, (35:22), we learn of another sorrow in Jacob's life. His first born son, Reuben, had intercourse with his father's concubine, Bilhah, who had been Rachel's handmaid. Jacob heard of it, but we are not told of his reaction until chapter 49:3, 4, when he gives his deathbed blessing to his sons. His words to Reuben were not blessing. As firstborn, Reuben had the birthright, but Jacob deprived him of that status. By his sin, he forfeited his birthright privilege. This is recorded in Israel's history in I Chron. 5:1. Jacob must have grieved the failure of his firstborn son.

Added to these sorrows, sometime after Jacob arrived back in Hebron, his father, Isaac, died.

CHAPTER SIXTEEN

A Chosen Teenager
Gen. 37

We have come to the place where the story of Jacob must merge with that of Joseph, for their lives intertwine through the rest of Genesis, as God's program moved forward.

Having at last come to Hebron where his father lived, Jacob settled in that area, and the story of Joseph begins.

> "These are the generations of Jacob. Joseph, being seventeen years old, was feeding the flock with his brethren; the lad was with the sons of Bilhah, and with the sons of Zilpah, his father's wives: and Joseph brought unto his father their evil report"

Joseph has always been regarded as one of the most godly and Christ-like characters in the Bible, a shining light of faith and righteousness. In recent times however, many have attempted to make him more "human" by assigning fault to him in many ways.

In the past, Joseph was considered to be an exemplary character: faithful to God under trial, honest and loyal in service to his Egyptian master, pure in the face of sexual temptation, submissive to the role God had given him to save Egypt and his family during famine, uncontaminated by his exile in pagan Egyptian society, and loving and forgiving his brothers, who had so cruelly betrayed him. These qualities have inspired generations, both young and old.

More recently, Joseph's so-called faults have been emphasized rather than his virtues. His important role in God's plan has been diminished as teaching concentrates on the details of his life in order to draw moral lessons from his perceived sins. His beautiful character and faith have been largely covered up by negative emphasis.

Three main points of criticism have been brought against Joseph. Most of the blame for these have been laid upon Jacob.

He was a tattletale who told on his brothers.
He was a braggart about his dreams.
Jacob's favoritism made Joseph a "spoiled brat".

Let us consider the record with an open mind and see if there is basis for these charges. Contrary to the opinion of one noted author, Joseph was not pampered to be idle. At the time he is introduced, he was helping to care for the family flocks in the field, learning the family occupation of animal husbandry. He was sharing this duty with his older half brothers, the sons of his father's secondary wives, who had more reason to be jealous of him than the others.

He reported their misconduct to his father, but we are not told what their misdeeds were. All the older brothers had proved, and would further prove, to be capable of some very evil deeds which were harmful to the family welfare.

Before we can justly label Joseph a petty tattle-tale, we would need to know what the evil report consisted of. It might be that the four brothers were doing something which was critical to the well being of the family. There is petty tattling, and then there is legitimate reporting of dishonest or dangerous behavior. Small children often tattle on each other. This is not what scripture is telling us about Joseph.

There are occasions when it is a duty to report evil conduct. Many a tragedy could have been avoided had someone had the courage to speak up. A son reports to his parents that his sister is doing drugs. Would he be considered a tattletale? No one likes to have his wrong doing exposed, but sometimes it is a kindness.

There is nothing in the account to suggest that Joseph was acting in the spirit of a tattletale. It was the brother's conduct which was evil, not Joseph's reporting. How often something is read into scripture which is not there.

> "And Joseph dreamed a dream, and he told it his brothers; and they hated him yet the more" (37:5).

Joseph has been unjustly accused of bragging about his dreams. However, there is nothing in these words to imply that he bragged, nothing to suggest that he told them his dreams with a proud attitude. For some strange reason, there tends to be a negative and judgmental mind-set toward Bible characters which leads to finding fault where none exists, and to infer blame where the sacred writers intended none. Joseph was not sinless, but there is no reason to read into the story faults which are not there.

Joseph had two dreams which perhaps perplexed him. In the first dream the family was binding sheaves in the field, when his sheaf stood upright and the other sheaves bowed down to his. In the second dream, the sun, moon, and stars bowed down to him. His brothers, and even his father, did not like the implication of the dreams that the family would all bow to him. Jacob reproved him, perhaps for the same reason he is criticized today, thinking he was arrogant. But something about the dreams rang true in Jacob's spirit; he had already sensed the hand of God upon the boy. "His father observed the saying" (v11).

This calls to mind Mary, who kept in her heart the puzzling words of the young Jesus, "Know ye not that I must be about my father's business?" Neither Mary nor Jacob understood the full implication of their young sons' words, but each felt a prophetic import, which was no doubt recalled at a later time. Young Joseph was also being called to his heavenly Father's business.

Joseph was immature and unwise to tell his dreams if we judge it from the natural viewpoint. It was certain to cause resentment. But Joseph was not lording it over his brothers in pride or desire for preeminence. His dreams were prophetic in nature, and prophecy is given to be proclaimed. The brothers just happened not to like the subject of this prophesy.

Prophesies are given ahead of the events they foretell, so that when they come to pass, those involved will be able to recognize that God is in the circumstances. As Jesus said: "I have told you before it come to pass, that, when it is come to pass, ye might believe" (John 14:29). Joseph was *supposed* to tell his dreams, so his family would later remember that these things were foretold, and believe that God was directing their lives.

Later, in Egypt, the fulfillment of the dreams showed that Joseph would be exalted to a high position, not that he might rule over them, but he would have authority and power to give them a place of refuge and provision during the famine. He did not become their lord, but from his position of influence he could be their benefactor. Jacob did not literally bow down to his son; but the guilty brothers did obeisance to him more than once.

The record says frankly, "Now Jacob loved Joseph more than all his children, because he was the son of his old age; and he made him a coat of many colors" (37:3). The fact that Joseph was the firstborn of Rachel, the only woman he ever truly loved, would also explain his special love for Joseph. Usually, one point is made from this verse. Moral lessons are drawn at great length about the evils of parental favoritism. It is a valid lesson, but there is more here than the common partiality of a parent for a certain child.

In our society, parental favoritism is strongly condemned. However in other cultures and times, one son was customarily designated as heir, and given special treatment. Consider the royal family of Britain; the eldest son inherits the throne. This is not a matter of favoritism. Bible commentators tell us that the special robe most likely indicated that Jacob planned to make Joseph head of the clan. Later, he did in fact give the birthright to Joseph, with good reason.

We have already seen that some of the other sons had proven unworthy of the birthright position. Reuben, the firstborn, forfeited his birthright because of sin. Simeon and Levi, who were next in line, were also denied the birthright privileges because of their cruel vengeance upon the Shechemites, which dishonored Jacob's name and Jacob's God.

I Chron. 5:1, 2 confirms in the sacred records of Israel that Reuben was displaced by Joseph for the birthright; however, rulership was passed on to the fourth son, Judah. Jacob was clearly following divine leading when he favored Joseph.

In this special love for Joseph, Jacob was moved not only by ordinary human emotions; he was being influenced by the sovereign hand of God to accomplish purposes of which Jacob could see very little. Joseph was a chosen instrument for a special work.

Jacob must have sensed a special destiny for Joseph and he felt a spiritual kinship with this spiritual son. Joseph clearly had qualities of character far above those of his brothers. All the other sons, with the exception of Benjamin, at some time betrayed him, but Joseph was different.

Intent on seeing these incidents from the human viewpoint, we miss the divine perspective. This history of God's salvation Plan was not written to instruct us about the errors of parental partiality, although that is useful instruction. More value is to be found in the stories of the patriarchs when the big picture of what God is doing is the focus of our study, rather than the perceived faults and moral shortcomings of these people who were being used by God for larger purposes.

The experiences of the patriarchs need to be seen in the light of the covenant thread which is the real story in Genesis. If only the human aspects are seen and proper recognition is not given to the central theme, the basic meaning of the history can be missed.

It is not the faults of these spiritual forefathers, but their faith, which is the main theme in Genesis. The New Testament reflects this fact when speaking of Abraham, Isaac and Jacob or Joseph; their failings are never mentioned, only their faith (Heb. 11; Rom. 4).

By focusing on their shortcomings, their morals are made more important than their faith. Joseph was not only Jacob's choice, but he was chosen by God as well, to be a deliverer and protector of the chosen seed. The brothers' hatred of him was without excuse. It was one more instance of Israel's long pattern of rejecting their deliverers.

CHAPTER SEVENTEEN

The Cost of Being Part of a Larger Plan
Gen. 37: 12-36

We are familiar with the sad story of Joseph's being sold by his brothers into slavery, and their deliberate deception of their father, which led him to believe Joseph had been killed by a wild beast! It is interesting that in attempting to put an end to Joseph and his dreams, they only helped bring them to pass, and unwittingly contributed to the fulfilling of God's purposes.

Credit should be given to Reuben, the eldest brother, who endeavored to save Joseph by persuading the others not to kill him, but to cast him into a dry cistern. Reuben intended to return later, rescue Joseph, and return him to his father (vs 21, 22). However, his good intentions were foiled when during his absence, some Ishmaelite traders came along, giving the brothers the idea of selling Joseph to the traders, who were on their way to Egypt.

Judah also deserves some credit for suggesting they not kill their brother, but sell him. By this small evidence of conscience in Judah, Joseph's life is spared; and God's plan to use him to save his family and many others, during the coming famine, goes forward.

Splattering Joseph's special robe with goat's blood, they took it to Jacob, claiming to have found it; leaving the old man to draw the obvious conclusion that a wild beast had killed his son. Jacob went into deep mourning for many days, refusing to be comforted.

In this, the most profound tragedy in Jacob's life of many sorrows, he has been denounced for refusing to be comforted, because he said, "I will go down to the grave unto my son mourning". His expression of grief has been interpreted to mean that he descended into bitterness and lost his faith. This is only conjecture, however. We can either judge him here in the worst possible light; or we can apply the New Testament principle of weeping with those who weep.

Is it so wrong, in the first emotional anguish of the loss of a loved one, especially under tragic circumstances, to feel there is no balm sufficient to heal our sorrow? The death of a child is especially grievous. Is it faithless to feel that our grief will go with us for the rest of our life? Sometimes it does, even though the intensity of sorrow eases with time and we go on with our life.

If we want to make Jacob more human like ourselves, he should be allowed his very human grief, without condemnation. After all, this was the child of his beloved Rachel, whom he had also lost prematurely. "Thus he wept for his son", should arouse compassion rather than judgment.

Those who interpret the scriptures for us usually point out that just as Jacob deceived his father in the matter of the blessing, now he himself is deceived by his sons. He is reaping what he sowed. He is suffering chastisement for his sin. But is it not also claimed that when Laban deceived him by substituting Leah for Rachel, he was the victim of that deception because he himself had deceived?

This is now the second time Jacob has been the victim of cruel deception. It has been some thirty seven years since he deceived his father. Is he now paying the second time for that sin? One has to wonder just how many times he was made to reap the harvest of that one act. Is this how God works, to chasten His children over and over for the same mistake?

Is this how we interpret the circumstances of our own lives? If we have failed in the past, does every affliction thereafter mean we are reaping the harvest of that failure?

This desire to link Jacob's loss of Joseph with his having deceived his father has led some to observe that as he deceived Isaac with the skins of goats on his arms, so now he is deceived by the blood of goats on Joseph's robes. The principle of sowing and reaping is carried too far!

Jacob's life has been reduced to a series of chastisements for his sins, as though there were no other reason for life's misfortunes. He had more than his share of sorrows in his lifetime. However, to see all of life's trials and afflictions, Jacob's or our own, as the result of personal sin, is a mistaken view of life.

When we ourselves suffer some affliction or trial, we often try to understand it in terms of the Lord working in us to correct some fault or wrong attitude. Trials often do accomplish this. God does at times chasten His children for their good. But I suggest another possible way of viewing Jacob's trials, and perhaps our own.

Apart from Abraham, Jacob is the most significant character in Genesis in the development of the covenant people. He was not chosen and set apart only for his own salvation and the refining of his moral qualities. The circumstances of his life had broader purpose than simply the development of his character. They were part of a larger plan. If we see no further than Jacob as an individual, we will miss the import of the events in his life in their larger context.

God was sovereignly overseeing the working out of His Plan of the Ages; and Jacob was a preeminent part of that plan. When Joseph was taken from him, this was not related to any past failure on Jacob's part. It was engineered by the Lord for a greater purpose, as He positioned Joseph in high office in

Egypt, preparing the way for this covenant people, and Egypt as well, to survive the extended famine.

This was the immediate purpose. But think of the greater design. The stage was being set for one of the most amazing events in history, the Exodus; the emancipation of Israel from 400 years of slavery. This was an event which, some 3,000 years later still glorifies God and teaches about spiritual salvation. Surely there is more to Jacob's story than simply chastening one man or refining his character!

In this Gospel age the focus is properly on personal salvation and personal growth in holiness; however, the result of this is a tendency to lose sight of the larger picture—God's ultimate goal! The plan is to deliver the whole creation from the bondage of corruption, deliverance as big as the original catastrophe. This involves not only deliverance from sin, but from death and corruption. (Rom 8:19-23; II Pet. 3:13; Rev. 21).

Jacob, as well as Abraham, Moses, David, John the Baptist, Mary and Joseph, and Paul were not saved only to make sanctified saints of them personally, but to play their roles in God's eternal purposes. Whether we recognize it or not, each of us also has our own role to play, small or great.

Anyone called to this purpose will inevitably suffer. A sword would pierce Mary's soul (Lu. 2:35); Paul's ministry was costly in terms of personal affliction and suffering, even martyrdom; Jesus could not save the world apart from the cross. Carrying blessing to the world cannot be done without some trials. Not all trials are for the purpose of personal growth. Some are the cost of being part of a larger plan.

I submit that Jacob was not suffering for some past misdeed, but was experiencing the cost of being a servant of God; of being used for eternal purposes. Any parent who has experienced a child leaving home to go to a foreign mission field suffers that loss and separation for the sake of the kingdom. They understand this; Jacob had no way of knowing.

It can be said that Joseph was sent to Egypt as a missionary or ambassador for God. This was what he was born for; this was his life's purpose and mission. Of course, Jacob suffered as a result. Only after twenty-two years was he allowed to see and understand what God was doing in their lives, and why Joseph was taken from him. God meant it for good.

In New Testament language, God was working all things together for good to these men who were called according to His purpose (Rom 8:28) .

CHAPTER EIGHTEEN

Joseph Blooms Where He is Planted
Gen. 39-41

Joseph was seventeen when his brothers treach-erously sold him to the Ishmaelite traders going down to Egypt, where he became a slave in the house of Potiphar, an official of Pharoah. God was with Joseph and made everything he did to prosper, so that he was put in charge of all his master's affairs. As the Lord had blessed Laban for Jacob's sake, so blessing came upon Potiphar for Joseph's sake. The promise that all the world would be blessed through Abraham's seed was in this small measure already beginning, but when Potiphar's wife attempted to seduce the handsome young steward, and was refused, she cried rape, and Joseph was sent to prison.

Remembering his dreams, his faith must have been greatly tried. Instead of enjoying an exalted position, he found himself a slave, and then things got worse: he was imprisoned.

Suffering such injustice from his brothers, and now from Potiphar's wife, exiled in a strange and ungodly culture, cut off from family and home, utterly alone, yet seemingly without bitterness or self pity; he must have faced that big question which we all face at times...Why?

But Joseph bloomed where he was planted. He had served his master faithfully with honest hard work, being responsible and reliable, submitting to his situation of slavery, "with good will doing service as to the Lord and not to men" (Eph. 6:7). Now in prison, this same attitude brought him respect and trust, so that he was put in charge of the prison.

His godly character and attitude are revealed by his concern for his fellow prisoners. One morning he noticed that the butler and the baker from Pharaoh's house were looking sad. Asking why, he learned they had each had a dream and were concerned about the meaning of the dreams. Joseph assured them that God would interpret their dreams through him. The divinely inspired interpretations came true when the baker was executed and the butler was restored to his former position of service to Pharoah.

Though he asked the butler to mention him to Pharoah, the butler forgot Joseph for two long years, until Pharoah himself had two troubling dreams which his wise men and magicians were unable to interpret. It was then the butler remembered Joseph and told

Pharoah about the young Hebrew who could interpret dreams. His kindness to the butler was rewarded when he was summoned to stand before Pharoah.

With humility he acknowledged it was not in his power to interpret dreams, but his God would give the answer to their meaning. His faith and relationship with God were such that he could confidently expect the Lord to do just that.

Pharoah's dreams were a warning that after seven years of abundant harvest, there would come seven years of grievous famine. To this idolatrous king, Joseph witnessed to the true God who knows the future and controls it: "God has shown Pharoah what he is about to do".

Then, no doubt still under inspiration, he advised the great Pharoah to appoint a wise man over the land of Egypt, to collect and store food during the seven good years, to be drawn upon during the seven years of famine. Perhaps this was what the New Testament calls a "word of wisdom". (I Cor. 12:8).

Whereupon, Pharoah, also being moved by the Lord (Prov. 21:1), appointed Joseph, "a man in whom the spirit of God is", as overseer of all Egypt, promoting him to a position second only to Pharoah himself. Joseph was given a wife, who bore him two sons during those years of abundant harvest, and Joseph was placed in charge of collecting and laying up food and grain in preparation for the coming lean years of famine. He was thirty years old at this time.

God was sovereignly directing the affairs of men to accomplish His far- reaching purposes.

It is popular to see Joseph as his brothers did, a spoiled, bragging, tattletale. But everyone else, from his father to Potiphar, from the prison master to Pharoah, saw in him excellent and admirable qualities worthy of a man in whom the spirit of God dwells.

Now the thirteen years of servitude began to make sense, as Joseph realized that God was indeed with him, for only He could have lifted him so miraculously to the position in which he found himself. Who would have imagined that this young man possessed such gifts of organization and administration as were required for the incredible task assigned him? Perhaps he didn't possess them; perhaps they were indeed gifts.

Immersed in the idolatrous culture of Egypt, with no scriptures, no church, and no fellow believer, his faith remained strong and true. We get a glimpse of his inner spiritual life when we consider the names he gave his two sons. The firstborn he named Manasseh, meaning "forgetting", because God had helped Joseph forget his years of hardship and his father's house (not that he couldn't remember, but he had peace, knowing he was where God had placed him). The second son he called Ephraim, "fruitful", for the Lord had blessed him in his new life. He saw God in it all.

Reading about Joseph we can see that he was not at the mercy of circumstances with no meaning or purpose. It is more difficult to perceive this in our own trials, but we should not get discouraged or be depressed, but know that our lives have meaning and purpose as surely as Joseph's. God is working something good for us or perhaps something *through* us for the good of others.

CHAPTER NINETEEN

Unexpected Change
Challenges Faith
Gen. 42-46

When the seven good years came to an end and the famine began to be felt in Canaan, Jacob sent his sons, all but Benjamin, to Egypt to buy food. Thus it was that the brothers came before Joseph, bowing down to him, asking to buy grain and fulfilling Joseph's dream. By this time Joseph was about thirty- seven years old, dressed as an Egyptian, and speaking the language of Egypt, so he was not recognized by his brothers. But Joseph knew them and remembered his dreams.

Testing them to see if they had perhaps changed in character and attitude, he accused them of being spies. Allowing them to buy food, he demanded to hold one of them as hostage until they could return and bring their younger brother with them if they wanted more grain. Not knowing the official could understand them, they said to one another, "We are verily guilty concerning our brother, in that we saw the anguish of his soul, when he besought us, and we would not hear; therefore is this distress come upon us" (42:21). Their conscience was being awakened.

Keeping Simeon in prison while the others returned home, Joseph put them to another test. On Joseph's orders the brothers' money was secretly returned to them in their sacks of grain. Opening one of the sacks on the way home, they were filled with apprehension, recognizing that God was somehow dealing with them.

Arriving home they were shaken once more to discover that each man's money was in his sack, and they were more afraid. When there was need to return to Egypt for more grain, they reminded Jacob that it was necessary for Benjamin to go with them. We remember that Benjamin was Joseph's only full brother, both sons of the beloved Rachel. Jacob objected:

> "My son shall not go down with you, for his brother is dead, and he is left alone; if mischief befall him by the way in which ye go, then shall ye bring down my grey hairs with sorrow to the grave" (42:38).

The possibility of losing both of Rachel's sons was more than he could bear. Under necessity he relented and gave permission for Benjamin to accompany his brothers. As they prepared to go, Jacob had them take a present to the man in charge of selling the grain. They took balm, honey, spices, myrrh, nuts, and almonds. He also directed them to take double money: money to buy more grain, plus the money they had found in their sacks, in case it had been put there by mistake.

This incident belies the picture of Jacob portrayed as a greedy, dishonest cheat, always out to take advantage of others. If he were that kind of man, he would have taken advantage of the situation and kept the money. Much unreasonable vilification has been heaped upon this man of God. He sends generous gifts of such as he had, and returns the money found in the sacks in case it had been an oversight. This was the act of an honest upright man.

His quiet nature and submission to God shines through in his response to the heartbreaking situation in which he finds himself. Joseph is dead, Simeon is held prisoner in Egypt, and now Benjamin must accompany his half-brothers to Egypt. The heartbroken old patriarch does not know if he will ever see Benjamin again. In faith and quiet resignation he puts the situation in the hand of God with a prayerful blessing:

> "God Almighty give you mercy before the man, that he may send away your other brother and Benjamin. If I am bereaved of my children, I am bereaved" (43:14).

The brothers, with young Benjamin, appear once more before Joseph, still not knowing who he is, and are invited to his home for dinner. They present their gifts, bowing to him again, and enjoy a feast with him. Yet another test awaits them as they set out for home with both Simeon and Benjamin. Joseph instructed his servant to put his silver cup in Benjamin's sack. Before they had gone far, the servant overtakes them with the accusation that they had stolen the ruler's cup. Imagine their consternation when the cup is found in Benjamin's sack!

Returning to the city, they fall before Joseph, and Judah pleads eloquently on Benjamin's behalf, offering to take his place as a slave to the ruler. Seeing the evidence of change in his brothers, Joseph reveals his identity to them, weeping aloud. In the spirit of loving forgiveness, Joseph explains that it is all a plan of God:

"God sent me before you to preserve you a posterity in the earth, and to save your lives by a great deliverance. So now it was not you that sent me hither, but God" (45:7, 8).

They are urged to bring their father and all their families to Egypt where Joseph can provide for them during the remaining five years of famine. Even Pharoah himself encouraged the move and sent wagons to carry old Jacob, the wives and children. The good news that Joseph was alive was almost more than Jacob could believe, but he said:

"It is enough; Joseph my son is yet alive; I will go and see him before I die" (45:28).

Some Bible teachers have soundly condemned Jacob for going down to Egypt. Had not God commanded Isaac, his father, not to go to Egypt during the famine in his time? Are we to assume that this command applies to all God's people at all times? Is going to Egypt always out of the will of God? Evidently not, for Joseph and Mary were directed by God to take the young child Jesus and flee to Egypt to escape the intent of Herod to kill him. And the record makes it plain that Jacob's Joseph was divinely sent before his family to Egypt to preserve their lives there.

Jacob set out for Egypt with all that he had, but stopped at Beersheba, the southernmost city in Canaan, near the border. There he worshipped, offering sacrifices to the God of his father, Isaac. Why Isaac's God? Why not Jacob's God? Because, this move involved the covenant relationship with his fathers and with himself. The land of Canaan had been promised; why then was God leading in the direction of Egypt? This was an unexpected change in his life, testing his obedience and faith. He too, remembered the command to Isaac, so he worshipped and sought guidance. Was this momentous move really of God? As Jacob had not left Laban without a definite word from God, so he would not leave Canaan without assurance that he was in the will of God regarding this journey and the great change it meant in the life of his people.

This is what we should do in most instances. We begin moving in the direction in which Providence seems to be leading, but before committing to that course, we worship and seek God, giving Him opportunity to guide us. God responded to Jacob:

> "And God spake unto Israel in the visions of the night, and said, Jacob, Jacob. And he said, Here am I. And he said, I am God, the God of thy father, (the God of the covenant), *fear not to go down into Egypt*; for I will there make of thee a great nation: *I will go down with thee into Egypt*: and I will surely bring thee up again; and Joseph shall put his hand upon thine eyes" (46:2-4).

With this word from God, how can it be questioned whether Jacob was in the will of God in going to Egypt? Three times in his life he heard this reassuring promise from the Lord: "I will be with thee".

1) When he left Canaan fleeing from Esau (28:15)
2) When he left Laban to return to Canaan (31:3)
3) Upon leaving Canaan to go to Egypt (46:4)

At times of great change in our lives is when we need the assurance that God is with us, leading us in our journey of faith. The Lord kept His promise and was with Jacob throughout all those years, guiding him according to His purpose.

It was a touching reunion when Joseph came to meet his father and his family. Joseph fell on his father's neck and they "wept a good while". They had been through hard trials, but as Joseph had said to his brothers, "God meant it for good". It was all according to His long-range plan and purpose. These two men, humbly submitting to God's providential leading, allowed themselves to be used to accomplish that purpose, even though they suffered in doing so.

Now Jacob and his clan, under the protection and provision of Joseph, were given an area of Goshen, a fertile part of Egypt ideal for their flocks and herds. The brothers had indeed bowed down to him, not as their superior or lord, though he was in a position of authority, but as their representative and provider.

One has to wonder just when, and if, the brothers remembered Joseph's dreams and really understood how God had worked things for the good of all.

CHAPTER TWENTY

Faith is Passed On
Gen. 46:5-50:26

Joseph took his father and some of his brothers to present them to Pharoah, who welcomed them graciously and confirmed that they could dwell in the area of Goshen. With patriarchal dignity, old Jacob blessed the mighty Pharoah. It was a humble expression of appreciation for his gracious hospitality in allowing the clan to sojourn in Egypt during the remaining 5 years of the famine. In answer to Pharoah's respectful question, "How old art thou?" Jacob replied:

> "The years of my pilgrimage are a hundred and thirty. My years have been few and difficult, and they do not equal the years of pilgrimage of my fathers" (47:9 NIV).

His testimony was that his life was a pilgrimage, a sojourn in a world which was not his home. He had his eye on a better country, a heavenly. Whether in Haran, Canaan or Egypt, he felt himself an alien and a stranger, just passing through on his way to that eternal promised land. Like Abraham and Isaac, he had not received the promises, but had seen them afar off.

His hundred and thirty years were fewer than either Abraham's or Isaac's, and they truly had been difficult years. He was not complaining; he had indeed experienced many sorrows and trials. Now he was to enjoy seventeen more years in Egypt, living near his beloved Joseph.

Before leaving Pharoah's presence, Jacob, as a prophet, once more conveyed the blessing of God upon the ruler. It is usual for the lesser to be blessed by the greater; in this case, Jacob was the greater, the servant of God, blessing an earthly potentate. He had the authority to do this, for the Lord had promised to bless those who blessed these covenant people (12:3). Egypt had already been blessed with Joseph's inspired wisdom in dealing with the famine. Now the ruler receives further blessing from Jacob. The time would come when a new king would arise who did not know Joseph, and would begin to oppress God's people, but for that generation there was blessing.

As Jacob approached the end of his life, he called for Joseph with a special request that he not be buried in Egypt, but that he be carried out of Egypt to rest with his fathers in their burying place in Canaan. That was the land promised and his heart had always been there. His request was an expression of his faith. Though circumstances seemed to deny the possibility, he knew his descendants would, in due time, return and inherit that land, for God had promised.

Shortly after this, Joseph, upon hearing that his father was sick, brought his two sons to visit their grandfather. Israel strengthened himself and sat up on the bed, telling them about God's gracious hand upon his life, and the faithful promises made to him and to them.

"God Almighty appeared to me at Luz (Bethel), in the land of Canaan, and blessed me. And said unto me, Behold, I will make thee fruitful, and multiply thee, and I will make thee a multitude of people; and will give this land to thy seed after thee for an everlasting possession" (48:3, 4).

He passed on the promises and his faith in those promises, to the second and third generations. Then, in an interesting and significant ritual, Jacob adopted Joseph's two sons, Manasseh and Ephraim, making them equal to his own sons.

To understand the significance of this, we remember that the firstborn son, Reuben, had forfeited his birthright because of sin. The next two sons, Simeon and Levi, also lost their place in line by their sinful actions at Shechem. Therefore Jacob gave the birthright position to Joseph. In this way, Joseph received the double portion due to the eldest son. Each of Joseph's sons became a tribe among the twelve tribes of Israel. Therefore, there is no tribe of Joseph.

Some of Jacob's last thoughts and words were about his beloved Rachel, Joseph's mother. She had been dead many years, but his love for her endured a lifetime, for he was a man of deep and lasting love. How appropriate that this gentle and quiet man should speak to Joseph about his mother at this time(Gen.48:7). He was described in the beginning as a quiet man, a family-oriented man. Family was his chief concern all through his life, and even now on his deathbed, his concern is evident. He was well chosen to father God's special people, and to have them called by his name. His thoughts were focused on this unique family of his and their sacred relationship with the covenant God of their fathers. He was faithfully preparing them for the future.

His loving nature shines through as he kissed and embraced his two grandsons, and praised God that though he had thought he would never see Joseph again, God allowed him to live to see Joseph's sons. He was very much aware of the presence of the Lord in his life.

Joseph brought his two boys before Jacob, with the older Manasseh toward Jacob's right hand, expecting him to bestow the blessing of the firstborn upon him; however, Jacob, responding to the guidance of the Spirit, deliberately crossed his hands to lay his right hand upon the head of the younger Ephraim.

"Then he blessed Joseph and said, May the God before whom my fathers, Abraham and

Isaac walked, the God who has been my shepherd all my life to this day, the Angel who has delivered me from all harm—-may he bless these boys. May they be called by my name and the names of my fathers, Abraham and Isaac, and may they increase greatly upon the earth" (48:15, 16 NIV).

He refers specifically to their covenant relationship with the Lord and gives glory to God for His goodness to him. Long before the Psalmist spoke of the Lord as his shepherd, Jacob testified that God had shepherded him from birth til death, recognizing the hand of the Lord upon him even before he was born. He gave glory to the Angel who had delivered him from all harm in numerous instances; the Angel who had saved him from Laban's devious treatment, met him at Peniel and gave him his new name of honor; the Angel who saved him from Esau's wrath and from attack by the Canaanites after the massacre at Shechem. May this God who loved him, bless these two grandsons, who will carry the name of Jacob-Israel as they increase according to the promise.

When Joseph saw Israel place his right hand on the younger son, he objected, but Jacob refused to change, for he saw through inspiration that Ephraim would be greater than Manasseh. This was not an act of favoritism, but of inspirational insight given by the Spirit of God, who knows all things and sees the future.

This is just one of numerous instances where the youngest is given preeminence over the firstborn.

God is free to do as He pleases, to by-pass custom if He chooses.

> "Behold, I die; but God shall be with you and bring you again unto the land of your fathers" (48:21).

Ephraim and Manasseh were half Egyptian and had never seen Canaan. Jacob was instilling in them his faith and their heritage. This hope and assurance he left with them to carry them through the trying years of bondage ahead of them, that they might wait for God's deliverance and look to Him in faith.

Then Jacob called for all his sons so he could tell them what their future would be and to bless them. Beginning with the eldest, Reuben, he reminded him of what his potential had been as firstborn, had he not sinned. Simeon and Levi were the next two brothers. Referring to their cruel violence to the Shechemites, Jacob said, "Let me not enter their counsel, let me not join their assembly." He pronounces a curse, not on the sons themselves, but on their anger, and testified that he disassociated himself from their actions in that incident. He prophesied these two tribes would be scattered in Israel.

The fourth son was Judah, to whom Jacob, by inspiration, gave the leadership of the people. Thus he shared part of the birthright with Joseph.

> "The scepter shall not depart from Judah, nor the ruler's staff from between his feet, until

he comes to whom it belongs and the obedience of the nations is his" (49:10 NIV).

This is generally understood as a prophecy of
Christ, the Lion of the tribe of Judah. Blessings
were pronounced on each son, then for some reason,
Jacob-Israel pauses, and in v18 cries out to God: "I
have waited for your salvation, O Lord"; or perhaps
as some translations put it, "I wait for your salvation,
O Lord". Whatever was in his mind as he spoke of
the future of his descendants, his hope was fixed on
God's salvation to come.

There were special blessings for Joseph, and Jacob
said: "With bitterness archers attacked him; they shot
at him with hostility (referring to his brothers). But
his bow remained steady, his strong arms stayed
limber, because of the hand of the Mighty One of
Jacob, because of the Shepherd, the Rock of Israel"
(49:23, 24 NIV).

The mighty God of Jacob, who had strengthened
Joseph through his years of hard trials, would be his
Shepherd, and the Rock who would bless him and his
descendants after him.

He charged his sons not to bury him in Egypt,
but to carry him to the cave of Machpelah in Canaan,
where Abraham and Sarah, Isaac and Rebekah, and
Leah were buried. This was not a sentimental request,
but his witness of faith that Canaan would be their
future home. When first they had migrated to Egypt,
the assurance had been given, "I will surely bring
thee up again" (49:3, 4), meaning his whole people.
He died with total confidence in this promise.

Jacob-Israel was embalmed, and all Egypt spent 70 days in mourning. Scripture records a grand and impressive funeral for Jacob. Most of his family, as well as numerous Egyptian noblemen and elders, along with a large escort of chariots and horsemen, accompanied the patriarch to his final resting place, honoring the great man that he was. It was a funeral procession befitting a king.

Years later, when the time came for Joseph to die, he too, passed on the promises and his faith in God's word.

"I die: but God will surely visit you, and bring you out of this land unto the land which he sware to Abraham, to Isaac, and to Jacob. And Joseph took an oath of the children of Israel, saying, God will surely visit you, and ye shall carry up my bones from hence" (50:24, 25).

The great "faith chapter", Hebrews 11, singles out this particular act of faith by Joseph:

"By faith Joseph, when he died, made mention of the departing of the children of Israel: and gave commandment concerning his bones" (v22).

This last expression of Joseph's faith is perhaps the most significant of all. He passed on to the coming generations faith in the promises, reminding them that they were heirs of that covenant made with their forefathers. They were to wait for the certain deliverance of their God. So Joseph died, was embalmed, and put in a coffin in Egypt.

It has been said that the book of Genesis begins with "In the beginning God", and ends with "a coffin in Egypt", a sad ending of death and failure.

What a depressing view of this great book about the fathers of our faith and our God's unfailing faithfulness to his covenant people. It misses the point completely.

Joseph's coffin was a symbol of hope; a statement of faith in the faithful God of the covenant. When the children of Israel looked at Joseph's coffin, they were reminded of the promise of deliverance. They kept it unburied four hundred years in anticipation of that deliverance. Though their faith and expectation faded over time and through the stress of their bondage, that coffin remained as a symbol of God's sure promise.

God was true to His word. In His perfect time, He did visit them, bringing them out of Egypt with an amazing deliverance, and led them to the land He had promised. When they went out, they took Joseph's coffin with them, a triumphant symbol of the faithfulness of their God!

NOTES

1. Theodore H. Epp, THE GOD OF ABRAHAM, ISSAC, AND JACOB, (Back To The Bible Publishing,) Copyright 1970 by The Good News Broadcasting Association, Inc., Copyright transferred to Herbert W. Epp, 1991.

2. James Strong, STRONG'S EXHAUSTIVE CONCORDANCE OF THE BIBLE, 1988

3. Adam Clarke, CLARK'S COMMENTARY, Vol. 1, (Abingdon Press, New York, Nashville).

4. Launt, THE BARTERED BIRTHRIGHT, (E.P. Dutton, N.Y., N.Y. 1901).

5. THE NEW SCHAFF-HERZOG ENCYCLOPEDIA OF RELIGIOUS

KNOWLEDGE, (Baker Publishing Group, Grand Rapids, MI).

6. Gene A. Getz, JACOB, Following God Without Looking Back, (Nashville, TN, Broadman and Holman Publishers, 1960 Used by permission).

7. Oswald T. Allis, PROPHECY AND THE CHURCH, (P&R Publishing, Phillipsburg, NJ 1964).

8. Carl F. H. Henry, Consulting Editor, THE BIBLICAL EXPOSITOR, Genesis, H. C. Leupold, (Copyright 1960. Renewal 1988 Holman Bible Publishers. Used by permission.

9. Rawlinson, (ISAAC AND JACOB, 1890).

10. THE LAYMAN'S BIBLE COMMENTARY, Vol. 2, (Westminster John Knox Press, Louisville, KY).

11. R.T. Kendall, GOD MEANT IT FOR GOOD, (Morning Star Publications, Charlotte, North Carolina. Copyright 1986 by R.T. Kendall. Used by permission.

12. Francis Frangipane, THE THREE BATTLEGROUNDS, (Cedar Rapids, IA; Arrow Publications, 1989).

13. W. Graham Scroggie, THE UNFOLDING DRAMA OF REDEMPTION, The Bible As A Whole, (Zondervan Publishing House, Grand Rapids, MI, 1972).

LaVergne, TN USA
13 March 2011
219901LV00001B/45/A